INTRODUCING

Empiricism

Dave Robinson • Bill Mayblin

Edited by Richard Appignanesi

D0036618

Icon Books UK Totem Books USA

Published in the UK in 2004
by Icon Books Ltd.,
The Old Dairy, Brook Road,
Thriplow, Royston SG8 7RG
email: info@iconbooks.co.uk
www.iconbooks.co.uk

Published in the USA in 2004
by Totem Books
Inquiries to: Icon Books Ltd.,
The Old Dairy, Brook Road,
Thriplow, Royston
SG8 7RG, UK

Sold in the UK, Europe, South Africa
and Asia by Faber and Faber Ltd.,
3 Queen Square, London WC1N 3AU
or their agents

Distributed to the trade in the USA by
National Book Network Inc.,
4720 Boston Way, Lanham,
Maryland 20706

Distributed in the UK, Europe, South
Africa and Asia by TBS Ltd., Frating
Distribution Centre, Colchester Road,
Frating Green, Colchester CO7 7DW

Distributed in Canada by
Penguin Books Canada,
10 Alcorn Avenue, Suite 300,
Toronto, Ontario M4V 3B2

Published in Australia in 2004 by
Allen and Unwin Pty. Ltd., PO Box
8500, 83 Alexander Street, Crows
Nest, NSW 2065

ISBN 1 84046 545 X

Printed and bound in Singapore
by Tien Wah Press Ltd.

What is Empiricism?

THIS BOOK IS ABOUT EMPIRICIST PHILOSOPHERS WHO BELIEVE THAT HUMAN KNOWLEDGE HAS TO COME FROM *OBSERVATION*.

After all, we know about most things by seeing, hearing, smelling, tasting and touching them.

But none of these philosophers is quite sure what exactly that means.

MOST EMPIRICISTS THINK THAT IT'S QUITE POSSIBLE THAT ONLY *WE EXIST*, AND NOTHING ELSE.

Empiricism starts off sounding like commonsense, but ends up by being utterly strange. Why Empiricists think what they do, and how they got there, is what this book's about.

It begins with a hippopotamus.

Knowledge and Belief

I'm sitting at my computer, after a long day, beginning the first few pages of this book, when without any warning a huge, leathery hippopotamus walks into the room.

THEN I WAKE UP. I'VE BEEN DREAMING.

I LOOK AROUND ME, AND THE COMPUTER'S STILL HERE.

SO ARE ALL MY BOOKS, GLASSES, A JAR FULL OF PENS, AND A MUG OF COLD TEA.

THE SUN IS SHINING OUTSIDE, AND THE TREES ARE MOVING IN THE WIND.

Now I'm confident that I'm awake. Everything I see, hear, smell, touch and taste is real, *this time*. Knowing about the world through the senses is the most primitive sort of knowledge there is. I couldn't function without it. But is it possible that I am mistaken, just as I was about the hippopotamus? How certain can I be about my perceptions of trees, jamjars and that cup of cold tea?

Most people assume that the world is pretty much as it appears to them. They believe a cat exists when they see it cross the road. But philosophers are, notoriously, more demanding. They say that beliefs are plentiful, cheap and easy, but true knowledge is more limited, and much harder to justify. This is why philosophers normally begin by separating knowledge from belief.

I PERSONALLY BELIEVE IN THE CONTINUED EXISTENCE OF THIS ROOM AND THE GARDEN OUTSIDE, BUT NOT IN THAT HIPPOPOTAMUS.

I ALSO THINK MY BELIEFS ABOUT THE REALITY OF MY IMMEDIATE SURROUNDINGS ARE JUSTIFIED BECAUSE THEY SEEM NATURAL, NORMAL AND OBVIOUS.

That's enough to convert my beliefs into knowledge. But there is always a slight possibility that I am wrong. The world might not be as I believe it to be. Problems like these worry philosophers called "empiricists", because they think that private sensory experiences are virtually all we've got, and that they're the primary source of all human knowledge.

Inside and Outside

One thing we do know is that our senses sometimes mislead us. White walls can appear yellow in strong sunlight. Surgeons can stimulate my brain so that I "see" a patch of red that isn't there. I can have hippopotamus dreams, and so on. My sense experiences are at least sometimes created by my mind – or somehow *in* my mind. These comparatively rare "mistakes" have led many philosophers to insist that *all* my perceptions are "mediated".

WHEN I LOOK OUT OF THE WINDOW, AT THOSE TREES, IT SEEMS TO ME THAT I SEE THEM AS THEY ARE, DIRECTLY.

But I don't. What I see is a wonderful illusion created by my mind. Of course, I am totally unaware of that fact because my perceptions seem so natural, automatic and rapid. Psychologists tell me that what I actually see is a kind of internal picture, and they devise all sorts of tests and puzzles to prove it.

Originals and Copies

They say that the trees provide me with a "tree sensation" in my mind, and it's that which I see, not the trees themselves. If that is true, then all I ever see are "copies" of those trees, which I assume are very similar in appearance to the originals.

But, if I think about this even harder, then I realize I have no way of telling how accurate these copies are, because I cannot bypass my mind to take another "closer look" at the originals.

Perhaps the original trees are nothing like the cerebral "copies" at all, or worse still, don't even exist!

The more I think about perception, the weirder it becomes, and the more I realise that I must be trapped in my own private world of perceptions that may tell me nothing about what is "out there".

PERHAPS THERE'S JUST ME, AND NOTHING ELSE! SUDDENLY I FEEL DIZZY.

Questions Lead to Uncertainty

This kind of unnerving conclusion is typical of philosophy. You ask simple questions which lead to unsettling bizarre answers.

If there isn't, how can empiricist philosophers claim that all human knowledge comes from experience? If no one can ever be sure where "experiences" come from in the first place, how reliable are they?

To Begin at the Beginning

Empiricist philosophy is relatively new. Philosophy as such began very differently, with some ancient Greeks called "Pre-Socratic" philosophers who emphasized the **differences** between appearance and reality. They said that what we **see** tells us very little about what is **real**. True knowledge can only come from thinking, not looking. The first truly systematic philosopher, **Plato** (427–347 B.C.E.), agreed that empirical or sense knowledge is inferior because it is subjective and always changing.

I ONLY BELIEVE THOSE TREES ARE "BIG" BECAUSE THEY'RE SLIGHTLY TALLER THAN MY HOUSE. MY "KNOWLEDGE" OF THOSE TREES IS WHOLLY RELATIVE TO ME.

WHAT KIND OF KNOWLEDGE IS THAT? EMPIRICAL KNOWLEDGE CAN ONLY EVER BE A MATTER OF "OPINION" OR "BELIEF".

Plato turned to mathematics instead. Unlike my trees, numbers are abstract, immune from physical change, the same for everyone, and have a permanence, certainty and objectivity that empirical knowledge lacks. Plato believed that real knowledge had to be like mathematics, timeless and cerebral.

Aristotle and Observation

Plato's famous student, **Aristotle** (384–322 B.C.E.), disagreed. He thought that it was important to observe the world as well as do mathematics.

I TRIED TO SHOW HOW ALL NATURAL THINGS FUNCTION AS A RESULT OF THE DIFFERENT CAUSES THAT AFFECT THEM.

Aristotle was not a very methodical scientist by our standards. His observations were often tailored to fit his complex metaphysical theories. Much of what he called "physics" was proved wrong.

Medieval Scholasticism

Aristotle's works resurfaced via Arabic scholarship in 12th-century Western Europe and eventually dominated medieval intellectual life. Western scholars were overawed by the apparent intellectual superiority of Greek philosophy and timidly assumed that human knowledge was virtually complete.

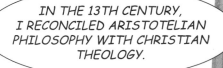

IN THE 13TH CENTURY, I RECONCILED ARISTOTELIAN PHILOSOPHY WITH CHRISTIAN THEOLOGY.

This strange synthesis devised by the Dominican cleric **St Thomas Aquinas** (1225–74) was subsequently taught in the medieval "schools" or universities and became known as "Scholasticism". Everyone imagined that philosophy and science had more or less reached a dead-end of perfection.

New Ways of Thinking

Medieval science was more concerned with words and definitions than systematic observation of the world. Attitudes began to change in the 16th and 17th centuries. The Reformation helped to loosen the grip of the Church on intellectual life. Modern scientists like **Johannes Kepler** (1571–1630) and **Galileo Galilei** (1564–1642) discovered that the universe was not at all as Aristotle had described it. The founder of modern philosophy, **René Descartes** (1596–1650), described an entirely new kind of science.

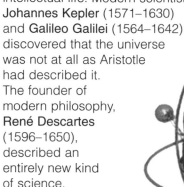

CERTAIN KNOWLEDGE DEPENDS ON INTROSPECTION WHICH RECOGNIZES A FEW "CLEAR AND DISTINCT" IDEAS AS NECESSARILY TRUE.

Descartes, like Plato, remained a "Rationalist" philosopher, convinced that scientific knowledge had to derive from mathematics and logic. He was nevertheless a major influence on empiricist philosophers.

The Cartesian model of the mind as a kind of "private room", and his corresponding theories of perception, reality, knowledge and certainty, seemed persuasive to most empiricist philosophers.

WE ONLY EVER PERCEIVE *PRIVATE IDEAS*, RATHER THAN THE OUTSIDE WORLD.

KNOWLEDGE HAS TO BE ASSEMBLED GRADUALLY, FROM THE *INSIDE OUT*.

Rationalists and Empiricists

Rationalist philosophers maintain that reason is the most reliable source of knowledge. *"Knowledge comes from thinking, not looking."*

Geometry provides the best systematic example of infallible, permanent knowledge based wholly on deduction. But empiricists" claim that, although geometrical and mathematical forms of knowledge are "necessary", they are only reliable because they are "trivial". Logic and mathematics do no more than "unpack" or clarify the inevitable consequences of a few preliminary definitions or axioms.

THE ANGLES OF A TRIANGLE *HAVE* TO ADD UP TO 180 DEGREES – IF YOU ACCEPT THAT THE SHORTEST DISTANCE BETWEEN TWO POINTS IS A STRAIGHT LINE, AND A FEW OTHER AXIOMS.

AND, IF ALL CATS HAVE WHISKERS, AND THIS IS A CAT, THEN IT MUST HAVE WHISKERS.

BUT THIS IS A CONCLUSION DERIVED FROM WORDS, NOT CATS.

T is for Triangle

They all have 180°

C is for Cat

All cats have whiskers

Logic and a Deeper Reality?

Empiricists say that neither geometry nor logic will tell you anything about the real world. The cerebral wonders of mathematics and logic are like chess – "closed" and "empty" systems constituted by their own sets of rules.

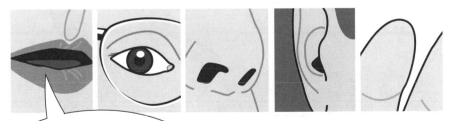

REAL KNOWLEDGE HAS TO ORIGINATE FROM SENSORY EXPERIENCES AS OUR ONLY GUIDE TO WHAT IS ACTUALLY TRUE.

There is no magical way of going beyond the limits of what we can see, hear, taste, smell and touch.

Later historians have often imagined a kind of "war" between the down to earth British "Empiricists" like Locke, Berkeley and Hume, and the more fanciful "Rationalist" continentals, like Descartes, Spinoza and Leibniz. But this controversy was not very real for those supposedly taking part. Few would have considered themselves stuck in either opposed "camp". The labels "Empiricist" and "Rationalist", although useful, can obscure the actual views of individual philosophers.

Francis Bacon

Francis Bacon (1561–1626) was a lawyer who eventually became Lord Chancellor. He was a corrupt politician, as well as a devoted scholar. He was obsessed with learning, of all kinds, and put forward several schemes for public libraries, laboratories and colleges. (The most famous is "Solomon's House" in his book *New Atlantis*.) Bacon believed in scientific progress, even though he was constantly aware of the limitations of human knowledge.

MEN MUST SOBERLY AND MODESTLY DISTINGUISH BETWEEN THINGS DIVINE AND HUMAN, BETWEEN THE ORACLES OF SENSE AND FAITH.

Bacon thought that a methodical and detailed observation of the world would massively increase the scope of human knowledge. It was only by studying the world's complex design that we would learn about its designer, God.

Empiricist Ants and Rationalist Spiders

Bacon was scathing about scholars who worshipped past "authorities" and obscured the "advancement of learning". Medieval "scientists" spent too long in libraries, arguing about definitions. Real science meant investigating the world outside.

It's all too easy for Empiricist "ants" to make haphazard and pointless collections of facts, or for Rationalist "spiders" to spin complex speculative theories out of nothing.

Scientific Bees and Induction

Successful "natural philosophers" are like sensible "bees". Their methodical collections of information stimulate theory, give rise to experiments, and produce the "honey" of scientific wisdom. Bacon devised a whole series of procedural methods for ambitious bee-scientists.

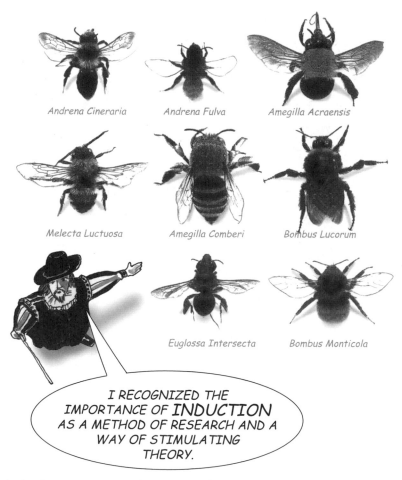

Andrena Cineraria   Andrena Fulva   Amegilla Acraensis

Melecta Luctuosa   Amegilla Comberi   Bombus Lucorum

Euglossa Intersecta   Bombus Monticola

I RECOGNIZED THE IMPORTANCE OF **INDUCTION** AS A METHOD OF RESEARCH AND A WAY OF STIMULATING THEORY.

Induction – as opposed to geometric deduction – means something like "drawing conclusions from the evidence". By observing many instances of the same phenomena (all sorts of bees make honey), we are able to draw probable conclusions (all bees make honey) and make predictions (these bees will make honey next year), and even emerge with explanatory theories for why things behave as they do (bees make honey in order to survive the winter months).

Bacon, Scientism and Thomas Hobbes

In Bacon's view, science was a moral activity. *"The 'New Philosophy' will produce great and marvellous works for the benefit of all men."* But he remains a propagandist for empirical methods, rather than a philosopher. He has little to say about the classic problems of empiricism. Nevertheless, after Bacon, it became harder for philosophers to dismiss empirical observations as trivial.

The young **Thomas Hobbes** (1588–1679) met Francis Bacon on several occasions and agreed wholeheartedly with this new "natural philosophy". Aristotelian ideas had to be abandoned in favour of a new "scientific" approach.

Hobbes was a radical materialist who declared that everything that exists must be physical – including minds and God himself (if He exists at all).

Hobbes was deeply impressed by the geometric method. From a few initial axioms, an extensive system of informative and certain knowledge could be deducted.

IF EVERYTHING IS PHYSICAL, AND THEREBY SPATIAL, THEN GEOMETRIC METHODS ARE THE BEST WAY TO CONSTRUCT A RELIABLE BODY OF SCIENTIFIC KNOWLEDGE.

Hobbes's *Leviathan*

Hobbes is best known for the political philosophy he espoused in his book, *Leviathan* (1651). He lived through the turbulent years of the English Civil War and the reigns of four monarchs.

> *I BECAME CONVINCED THAT HUMAN BEINGS ARE BORN SELFISH AND ARE ALL POTENTIALLY VIOLENT.*

LEVIATHAN,

OR The Matter, Forme, & Power,
OF A COMMON-WEALTH ECCLESIASTICALL AND CIVILL.

By THOMAS HOBBES of Malmesbury.

If there is no stable political society, then everyone quickly realizes that pre-emptive strikes are the best defence, a policy which quickly leads to social, economic and political chaos. The only remedy is a "social contract" between everyone, in which all agree to the appointment of a strong absolutist government to enforce law and order.

Hobbes the Empiricist

Hobbes always maintained that human knowledge has to come through sense experiences.

"There is no conception in a man's mind which has not at first, totally, or by parts, been begotten upon the organs of sense."

Sir Isaac Newton (1642–1727) was correct to describe matter as always in motion. Matter produces sensations in us, and these sensations in turn produce more internal motions of cerebral matter that we call "thoughts". This physical agitation of the brain becomes fainter if not periodically restimulated. Which means that memory and imagination are faint echoes of their originals or "decayed sense". Occasionally human thoughts are "unguided", but mostly they are motivated by the twin emotions of fear and desire, the primary driving forces behind all human behaviour and action.

OBJECTS IN THE WORLD ARE WHAT CAUSE HUMAN BEINGS TO HAVE THOUGHTS, AND OUR THOUGHTS ARE "REPRESENTATIONS" OF THOSE OBJECTS.

Human beings are able to express their thoughts and communicate through language. But language can also be a great deceiver, and persuade philosophers to believe in all kinds of metaphysical nonsense.

Locke and Empiricist Theory

John Locke (1632–1704), only a teenager at the time of the Civil War, was less absolutist in his political views. Nor was he an inflexible Hobbesian materialist. He thought that the mind couldn't possibly be a physical entity. This view made him, like Descartes, a "Dualist" who accepts two sorts of "substances" in the world – *material matter* and *immaterial minds*. Locke was the first philosopher to produce a systematic empiricist theory of perception, mind and knowledge. He concluded, in *An Essay Concerning Human Understanding*, that there are many things we cannot ever know, things about which we can only have beliefs.

IT IS NECESSARY TO SIT DOWN IN A QUIET IGNORANCE OF THOSE THINGS, WHICH UPON EXAMINATION, ARE FOUND TO BE BEYOND THE REACH OF OUR CAPACITIES.

But Locke was only a partial sceptic.

Innate Ideas on Blank Sheets

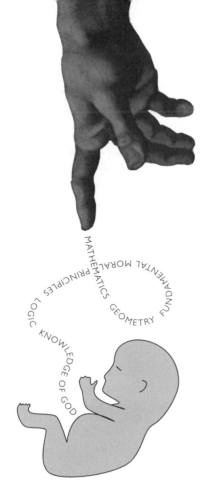

Locke's famous *Essay* begins with an attack on the doctrine of innate ideas. Rationalists like Plato and Descartes insisted that certain kinds of knowledge had to be *imprinted* on the human mind from the day we are born, or before. (Rationalist philosophers are usually enthusiastic innatists, because even they cannot create a philosophy out of nothing.) Some ideas cannot come from experience, especially those that are "obviously" true, like mathematics. Human beings are uniquely wired up to do mathematics and geometry.

God has stamped the idea of himself onto human minds, rather like a product trademark.

Neo-Platonists, in Locke's day, maintained that the elementary laws of logic, fundamental moral principles and a knowledge of God's existence had to be innate – how could such things ever possibly be observed?

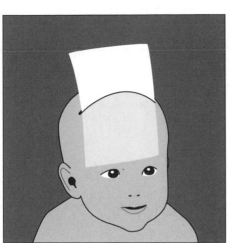

BUT I ARGUE THAT THE MINDS OF NEWLY BORN INFANTS ARE EMPTY, LIKE BLANK SHEETS OF WHITE PAPER.

The Empiricist Account

But if we aren't born with ideas, where do they come from? Locke resolves that knowledge must come through experience. We can only ever truly know those things that we experience for ourselves, not that which we take on trust. *"Such borrowed wealth, like fairy money, though it were gold in the hand from which he received it will be but leaves and dust when it comes to use."*

ALL OUR "IDEAS" MUST ORIGINALLY COME FROM SENSATION.

BUT THE MIND ONLY EVER ENCOUNTERS IDEAS – OR "OBJECTS OF THOUGHT" – NOT THINGS THEMSELVES.

This is the most important part of Locke's theory of perception and knowledge – we never experience the world directly. It's an odd assumption which informs the whole of Empiricist philosophy and often causes it immense grief. So we'd better look at it now.

Direct Realism

Most ordinary people are "direct" or "naive" realists, if you ask them about their everyday perceptions. They say that physical objects exist, are three dimensional, are independent of our perception of them and continue to exist when no one is looking at them. Physical objects are also "public" in that anyone can see them, unlike, say, dreams.

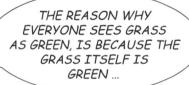

THE REASON WHY EVERYONE SEES GRASS AS GREEN, IS BECAUSE THE GRASS ITSELF IS GREEN ...

OUR PERCEPTION OF THE PHYSICAL WORLD IS ALL LIKE THAT – AN ACCURATE ACCOUNT OF WHAT'S OUT THERE.

BUT UNFORTUNATELY, IT'S NOT THAT SIMPLE.

Differences of Property and Experience

Put one hand in hot water, and one in cold, and then both in lukewarm water. The lukewarm water will feel warm to one hand and cool to the other. Water cannot be both objectively warm and cool at the same time, so our *experience* of the water cannot be a *property* of the water itself. Similar experiments involving sight, hearing, taste and smell all seem to demonstrate that perception involves many different factors, rather than just the intrinsic properties of things.

EVEN "SEEING" THAT GRASS IS GREEN TURNS OUT TO BE AN EXTREMELY COMPLEX PROCESS.

ELECTROMAGNETIC WAVES IN THE FORM OF WHITE LIGHT ILLUMINATE GRASS.

PART OF IT IS ABSORBED AND PART REFLECTED ...

... SPECIFIC WAVELENGTHS ENTER THE EYE, STIMULATE RETINAL CELLS, CAUSE COMPLEX CHEMICAL AND ELECTRICAL CHANGES IN OUR BRAINS ...

... AND END UP AT THE VISUAL CENTRE AT THE REAR OF OUR BRAINS.

"Greenness"

So we see with our brains. And, when we look at that grass, what we see is an internal "representation" of the world. And not everybody sees the green. Some people see our "green" as their "red".

Some animals see the world in black and white.

Some insects see much more than we do in the ultra-violet spectrum.

Our belief that grass is green is insecurely based on our own limited human perceptual apparatus.

WE ARE OTHER BEINGS WHO PERCEIVE THIS WORLD IN DIFFERENT WAYS TO YOU HUMANS, BECAUSE OF OUR DIFFERENT SENSE ORGANS.

27

Appearances Are All We Have

We tend to assume that we have a privileged insight into how things are. But our perceptions may be far less reliable than we think. Our "direct" experience of the world remains one that is mediated and disturbingly relative to us.

This means that we may have very little knowledge about what the world is like.

Appearances may be all we have. And if we know that our sensory experiences are sometimes unreliable, how are we supposed to know exactly when they **are** reliable, or whether they are reliable at all?

Responding to Scepticism

There are several responses you can make to these sceptical doubts. One is to say that, apart from a few rare and misleading exceptions, our experience of the world is direct and correct, a view which seems like bad science and rather anthropocentric.

ANOTHER IS TO SAY THAT PERHAPS WE CAN *NEVER* KNOW WHAT THE WORLD IS "REALLY LIKE".

We're permanently trapped in some kind of private multi-sensory cinema that bombards us with information. Some of it may be entirely correct or only partially true, and some wholly misleading. And we've no way of knowing which is which, because we have no direct contact with the world.

Representative Realism

Locke's apparently sensible compromise is to say that there are physical objects out there and that they are the cause of our experiences. After all, our experiences have to come from somewhere. This also explains why they are involuntary and continuous.

SO, ALTHOUGH WE CAN ONLY EVER EXPERIENCE MENTAL "REPRESENTATIONS", WE CAN BE FAIRLY SURE THAT THEY ARE ROUGHLY ACCURATE COPIES OF THE THINGS THAT CAUSED THEM.

For most people, none of this is of much importance, so long as their mental images of the physical world remain fairly constant and predictable. But for philosophers, especially empiricists, this uncertainty is a major worry, especially if you insist that all knowledge comes from experience.

Mental Images

But, what are we all experiencing exactly? Is it possible to base a whole system of knowledge on something as temporary and private as internal mental images which may, or may not, be copies of something else?

I WAS ALL TOO AWARE OF THESE KINDS OF PROBLEMS.

Locke seems to have ended up as a rather reluctant "representative realist". He thought that there probably were physical objects existing in the world, but he was sceptical about how much we could truly know about them. He attempts to account for our build-up of knowledge by its derivation from simple to complex ideas.

31

Simple Ideas

Let's go back to that infant with the empty mind. Where does its knowledge come from? If there are no innate ideas, then its mind must be totally blank. But, very quickly, its sensory organs begin to fill its mind with all sorts of "simple" ideas. This is how it acquires ideas of yellow, white, heat, cold, soft, hard, bitter, sweet, and so on. Other ostensibly "simple" ideas are those of space, size, shape, unity, power and succession, pleasure and pain.

MY "SIMPLE" IDEAS ARE "SIMPLE" IN A RATHER SPECIAL SENSE.

RED

THEY ARE SIMPLE BECAUSE THEY ARE EXTREMELY PRIMITIVE AND CANNOT BE "BROKEN DOWN" INTO OTHER IDEAS.

They are like the elementary pieces of the jigsaw puzzle that gradually assemble to create its infant knowledge.

Mental Jamjars

A child at first receives these simple ideas passively and involuntarily as if its mind were a container. It cannot control or invent these ideas, which, for Locke, suggests that there must be something real, outside of us, causing them to occur. And simple ideas can only ever be derived from experience.

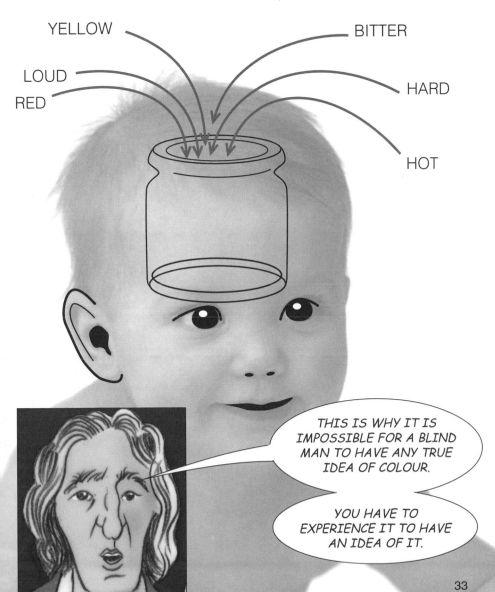

YELLOW

BITTER

LOUD

HARD

RED

HOT

THIS IS WHY IT IS IMPOSSIBLE FOR A BLIND MAN TO HAVE ANY TRUE IDEA OF COLOUR.

YOU HAVE TO EXPERIENCE IT TO HAVE AN IDEA OF IT.

Complex Ideas

Simple ideas are the building blocks of knowledge. Once they are stored in memory, however, the mind can become much more active. Locke envisages the mind at work: copying, selecting and reassembling simple ideas, rather like bits of Lego. This is how the mind makes its own new "complex" ideas – by thinking, doubting, reasoning, comparing, connecting and abstracting. No matter how complex or seemingly "abstract" our ideas eventually become, they must still ultimately be based on the simple ideas of experience.

Problems of Reflection

Locke offers a mechanistic explanation of the workings of the human mind, and is not always convincing. He has to admit to many innate abilities in the human mind for these complex processes of "reflection" to occur. We couldn't make much sense of our experiences, even the most "simple" ones, without some kind of preliminary conceptual apparatus.

It's more complicated than it looks.

It's also hard to see how absolutely **all** ideas can be ultimately based solely on experience – ideas like "weed", "risk", "tomorrow" and "debt", for example, as well as the grander concepts of time, space, mathematics, ethics and God.

Primary and Secondary Qualities

And, if all we ever experience are "ideas", how does Locke know that our "physical object ideas" are a reasonably accurate copy of things in the world?

It's possible we could be sure that physical objects are the cause of all our **experiences**, and yet still know nothing about their real **appearance**.

I COMPROMISE BY SAYING THAT WE CAN PROBABLY KNOW SOME THINGS FOR CERTAIN ABOUT PHYSICAL OBJECTS, BUT NOT EVERYTHING.

ONLY THOSE "IDEAS" OF THE MECHANICAL PROPERTIES (OR "PRIMARY QUALITIES") OF THINGS CAN PROPERLY BE THOUGHT OF AS EXACT RESEMBLANCES.

The Philosophy of Corpuscles

Locke's theories about perception and the physical world were influenced by the ancient Greek "atomist" philosophers and the "corpuscularian philosophy" of Locke's contemporary, the scientist **Robert Boyle** (1627–91).

THE PHYSICAL WORLD IS MADE UP OF TINY, ALMOST INVISIBLE "CORPUSCLES" WHICH HAVE ONLY "PRIMARY" QUALITIES OF SOLIDITY, SHAPE, SIZE, MOTION AND NUMBER.

THESE GIVE ANY OBJECT ITS MEASURABLE SIZE, WEIGHT AND SHAPE.

And these "ideas" of primary qualities are an accurate reflection of the physical objects themselves. Our idea of a ball's roundness resembles something intrinsic. The roundness is out there; we can know it to be true and measure it.

Secondary Qualities

Boyle noticed that objects also had other more mysterious "powers" or "secondary qualities" that stimulate our senses and brains in other ways. Locke agreed with the "modern" theory that physical objects emitted tiny particles that affected our sense organs. This is how primary qualities produced secondary ones. But exactly how physical phenomena can cause mental phenomena remained unclear, as it does to this day.

We experience other "secondary" ideas of colour, taste, smell and sound, besides those primary ones of shape and weight. But these secondary ideas of ours do not resemble anything that resides in the objects themselves.

DARK GRE

LIGHT GREEN

SMELL OF MOWN GRASS

NOISE OF LAWN MOWER

WHIRRRR

OUR IDEA OF GREEN IS NOT IN THE GRASS.

SO THIS TIME, OUR "IDEAS", OR PERCEPTIONS, ARE SOMETIMES DIFFERENT FROM THEIR CAUSES.

Subjective Objects of Sense

Secondary properties are not measurable, partly because they appear to be a strange mixture of objective physical powers and subjective mental experiences.

A red ball has no inherent redness, only a "power" to produce a human "red experience".

THE PHYSICAL WORLD IS, IN FACT, RATHER DULL – GREY, TASTELESS AND SILENT. IT IS WE HUMAN BEINGS THAT MAKE IT COLOURFUL, SMELLY AND NOISY.

Modern science now talks about photons instead of corpuscles, and we now know a lot more about how the external world affects our senses. But Locke still seems right to insist that there is a huge difference between measurable wave motions in the air and our uniquely human experience of *sound*, and quantifiable light wavelengths and our uniquely human experience of *colour*.

Substances Underlying Qualities

When we experience ideas they tend to congregate in groups – like the redness, shape, texture, smell and size – all perhaps produced by the physical object we call "an apple". Locke thought we were "predisposed" to respond to these clusters of properties as "things". At first he entertained the thought that perhaps physical objects had no inner "substance" or "a something we know not what" holding these qualities together in groups.

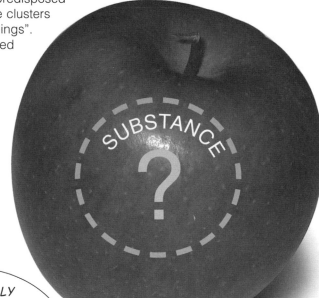

SUBSTANCE ?

BUT I FINALLY CONCLUDED THAT IT WAS HIGHLY IMPROBABLE THAT QUALITIES JUST FLOATED ABOUT IN BUNDLES ...

THEY HAVE TO ADHERE IN SOME WAY TO SOME SORT OF CENTRAL "SUBSTANCE" OR MATTER, EVEN THOUGH SUCH STUFF CANNOT BE DETECTED EMPIRICALLY.

So, although Locke thought it was material objects that affected human minds, their inner nature remained a complete mystery.

The Word "Idea" and Concepts

Locke tried to give an account of the complex causal processes that existed between objects, corpuscles and minds, and attempted to close the gaps – with "ideas". But his rather liberal use of the word "idea" is often confusing. The word "idea" was originally used in the 17th century as a synonym for "picture" and included mental imagery. Locke uses this one word to describe all sorts of very different mental phenomena – such as the immediate perceptions of objects, the introspective awareness of thoughts and feelings, the application of concepts, imaginations, memories, and so on.

IDEA OF AN ORANGE

I AGREED WITH DESCARTES THAT KNOWING SOMETHING IS LIKE "SEEING" AN OBJECT IN THE MIND.

But ideas are not "objects" in the normal sense of the word. The idea of an orange has no particular size and is not itself orange-flavoured.

Concepts as Images

Locke also talks about concepts as if they were internal mental images. But concepts are more like "dispositional abilities". When we possess concepts we are able to make judgements about our experiences.

"SEEING A RABBIT" INVOLVES EXPERIENCING A SET OF SENSORY IDEAS AND THEN IMPOSING THE CONCEPT OF "RABBIT" ONTO THEM ALL.

Many of these problems tend to diminish if you conceive of thinking as having more to do with language than pictures.

Words represent something other than themselves, and yet don't have to resemble what they "stand for". Locke would no longer then have to explain how an idea could be "coloured", for example.

Looking and Thinking

Locke's model of perception characterizes the instant process of perception as something more conscious and deliberate than it actually is. According to Locke, we receive visual information and then, by using our reason, make inferences about it. But this is not how we perceive the world.

WE GRASP PERCEPTUAL EXPERIENCES AS A WHOLE, NOT AS DISCRETE GROUPS OF DIFFERENT SENSATIONS.

OUR CONTACT WITH THE WORLD MAY BE MEDIATED BUT ALWAYS SEEMS DIRECT AND INSTANTANEOUS.

Locke is not clear whether he thinks of the processes of perception as *causal* or *judgmental*. It may be true that we only ever experience ideas, caused by physical objects, but our interpretation of this raw data is mostly automatic and unconscious. When I "see the trees" outside my window, I am unaware of the complex mental processes involved.

Language as Ideational

Locke was critical of philosophy expressed in empty, vague or ambiguous language. His theory of language is usually known as "ideational" because he maintained that words get their meaning by standing "as marks for the ideas within the mind".

THE RABBIT ...   EATS ...   THE APPLE.

WORDS ARE A SURROGATE FOR IDEAS. COMMUNICATION WORKS BY TRANSFERRING PRIVATE IDEAS FROM ONE MIND INTO ANOTHER.

This is a doubtful notion of how people communicate or how language gets its meaning. When we think or speak to someone, our words don't seem to be accompanied by a stream of parallel visual images.

...erstood that most words are general terms that refer to ... things. "Dog", "man", "giraffe" and "house" do not refer to particulars but to groups of things. We only experience particulars in the world. Generalities must therefore exist ...he mind. No one ever has an experience of a whole class. ... these ideas get into the mind? How do words refer to all the ... such a class? Locke's answer is that the mind creates ...deas. Abstraction is the ...uman process of seeing ...ces, separating out ...features from ...s" and then forming ...ideas.

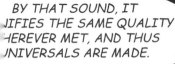

...AME COLOUR
... TODAY IN CHALK
... WHICH THE MIND
...ECEIVED FROM MILK,
... THAT APPEARANCE
...E THE NAME
...HITENESS.

... BY THAT SOUND, IT
...IFIES THE SAME QUALITY
...HEREVER MET, AND THUS
...NIVERSALS ARE MADE.

...deas are a bridge between ...things and general words, ...to explain how language ...you are a committed ...list".

Nominal and Real Essences

Locke's theories of linguistic meaning are also an account of how we classify our experiences. Although the world appears to be neatly pre-arranged into specific classes of things, in reality, thought Locke, it is we who do the classifying for reasons of convenience. Aristotle maintained that the world was already classified into "natural kinds". This meant that Aristotelian schoolmen could claim to know everything about gold by describing its outward appearance and behaviour. But they were only laying down a set of criteria for recognition. Such "nominal essences" are trivial in Locke's view and different from gold's "real essence" which consists of the metal's actual "substance" – its internal and invisible arrangement of minute particles.

YOU CANNOT KNOW A CLOCK BY DESCRIBING ITS APPEARANCE IN GREAT DETAIL.

BUT A CLOCKMAKER KNOWS ALL ABOUT THE INTERNAL ARRANGEMENTS OF COMPLEX COGS AND WHEELS, AND HOW IT REALLY WORKS.

Identity in Time

My motorbike is extremely old. So many of its parts have been replaced that it's debatable whether it's the "same" motorbike I bought some fifteen years ago. Locke was interested in this sort of "identity through time".

AM I THE SAME PERSON THAT I WAS 30 YEARS AGO?

WHAT ARE THE DIFFERENCES BETWEEN THE IDENTITY OF THINGS AND ANIMALS, AND THE PERSONAL IDENTITY OF HUMAN BEINGS?

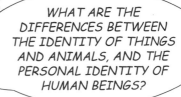

Minds and bodies occupy the same bits of space and time (rather fortunately, because they are made of different substances). A heap of gravel is not the "same" heap once a stone has been removed or added. Organic beings, like a tree or a fox, remain the same, even though they grow bigger than their earlier selves, because both have a specific kind of tree or fox "structure".

Personal Identity

The same is true of human beings as a species, but not of individual persons. A person remains the same if their consciousness persists. Memory and personal history make you the person you are. As is often the case with this philosophical problem, Locke explores it by looking at "puzzle cases".

IF THE CONSCIOUSNESS OF A PRINCE WERE TRANSFERRED INTO THE BODY OF A COBBLER, THEN THE PRINCE WOULD REMAIN HIMSELF ...

... EVEN THOUGH HE LOOKED DIFFERENT.

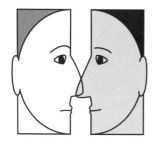 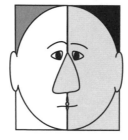

If there were two consciousnesses in one body, there would be two persons in one body.

Someone who had total amnesia might not, therefore, be the "same" person as before. For Locke, personal identity doesn't rely on bodily continuity, or even souls.

Locke's Politics

Because nobody can claim to know the whole truth about anything, Locke is critical of those who think they know all the answers, moral or political – hence why he was an advocate of religious and political tolerance.

I AGREED WITH HOBBES THAT GOVERNMENTS ARE NECESSARY, BUT ONLY BECAUSE LIFE WITHOUT THEM IS "INCONVENIENT" RATHER THAN UNSPEAKABLY AWFUL.

Governments are the neutral judges that can prevent endless vendettas and civil war. But citizens have rights (to property, especially) that pre-date governments. They must consent to being governed and retain the right to rebel against tyranny, something that Hobbes would never have allowed.

The Legacy of Locke's Empiricism

Locke was one of the first thinkers to "disenchant" Western philosophy from medieval tradition and ecclesiastical authority by advocating empiricism.

He produced a coherent account of the useful knowledge that can be gained from the senses, although he agreed with Descartes that it could never offer the cast-iron guarantees of mathematics and logic. He was a pragmatic representative realist, whose arguments about the way we perceive the world paradoxically stimulated all those "idealists" and "phenomenalists" who followed him.

AND THE INFLUENCE OF HIS POLITICAL THOUGHT ON ENGLISH, AMERICAN AND FRENCH POLITICAL HISTORY HAS BEEN IMMENSE.

Was He Right?

Modern genetics shows us that the human mind is far from "blank" at birth. It is also much more mysterious and less "open" than Locke thought. We do not think by inspecting entities, ideas, visual images or copies in the mind. We seem to be programmed as language-users. Language involves much more than the communication of ideas since it also partly determines how we conceptualize our experiences of the world. And, ultimately, Locke remains unable to prove conclusively that there is an independent external reality beyond my ideas.

IF MY EXPERIENCE OF MY CAT SITTING ON THIS TABLE IS CAUSED BY IT GIVING OFF PARTICLES WHICH ENTER MY EYES THAT CREATE "CAT IDEAS" IN MY MIND ...

... HOW CAN I KNOW THAT THESE "CAT IDEAS" ARE EVEN PART COPIES OF SOME REAL THING, OR THAT THE ORIGINAL CAT EXISTS AT ALL?

How do I know that the cat is one discrete physical object, composed of a core substance supporting properties of size, shape, blackness, smelliness and purring? What if it's just the properties themselves that I experience? That's where George Berkeley comes in.

The Prodigy

George Berkeley (1685–1753) was born near Kilkenny in Ireland. His father was English, but Berkeley always thought of himself as Irish. He was something of a child prodigy. He was only 15 when he went to Trinity College, Dublin, and he wrote his most famous philosophical works in his twenties: *An Essay Towards a New Theory of Vision* (1709), *A Treatise Concerning the Principles of Human Knowledge* (1710) and *Three Dialogues Between Hylas and Philonus* (1713). (Philonus means "lover of mind" and Hylas means "matter".) Berkeley made several journeys to Europe.

IN FRANCE, I MET THE PHILOSOPHER **NICOLAS MALEBRANCHE** *(1638–1715).*

I ALSO WENT TO AMERICA, WHERE I HOPED TO FOUND A UNIVERSITY, BUT RETURNED SOON AFTERWARDS TO IRELAND.

Berkeley eventually became Bishop of Cloyne, a post he held until he died. In the last 30 years of his life, he wrote many books and articles about religion, economics and the efficacy of "tar water" as a cure-all.

Berkeley's Aims

From the start, Berkeley claimed that he wrote both to defend commonsense and to protect religion against atheism. He knew a great deal about the new scientific and materialist world picture of Galileo, Newton and Robert Boyle that had convinced Locke. The Universe was a huge machine and God was a remote divine Being who imparted motion to all this astronomical machinery – and then abandoned it to run its course. Some philosophers even suggested that God might no longer be present to watch over his celestial clockwork.

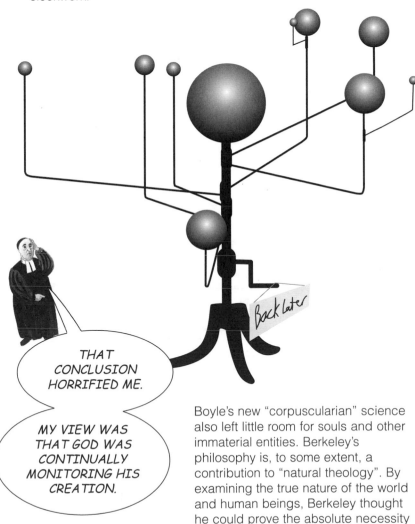

Back later

THAT CONCLUSION HORRIFIED ME.

MY VIEW WAS THAT GOD WAS CONTINUALLY MONITORING HIS CREATION.

Boyle's new "corpuscularian" science also left little room for souls and other immaterial entities. Berkeley's philosophy is, to some extent, a contribution to "natural theology". By examining the true nature of the world and human beings, Berkeley thought he could prove the absolute necessity of God's presence.

Ending in Scepticism

Berkeley reckoned that Locke's account of perception and knowledge must inevitably end in universal scepticism. If there was an unbridgeable gap between what our sensory experiences told us and what the external world was really like, then this would lead us to doubt everything.

> *HENCE WE SEE THAT PHILOSOPHERS DISTRUST THEIR SENSES, AND DOUBT OF THE EXISTENCE OF HEAVEN AND EARTH, OF EVERYTHING THEY SEE AND FEEL, EVEN OF THEIR OWN BODIES.*

The way forward, Berkeley thought, was to refute materialism utterly. By proving that appearance **is** reality, he could eliminate the unnecessary divide between them. Only our ideas exist, and nothing else.

Berkeley's Idealism

Berkeley agreed with Locke that we never perceive the world directly. All we experience is our own private mental imagery. Locke concluded that the existence of a physical world was probable if not provable. Berkeley was more radical: anything that cannot be perceived is not just unprovable but cannot exist. Locke's theory of perception involved three entities – minds, ideas and things. The mind has ideas which are caused by things. Berkeley drops "things". Existence is left only to minds and ideas. Whatever exists is mental.

THERE ARE NO TREES OUTSIDE MY WINDOW, ONLY MY SENSE EXPERIENCES OF TREES, WHICH ARE NOT "COPIES" OF "ORIGINALS". I ONLY EVER HAVE SENSE EXPERIENCES OF TREES, OR "TREE-LIKE EXPERIENCES".

This is why Berkeley is known as an "Idealist" (only ideas exist) or an "Immaterialist".

Esse est Percipi

To begin with, Idealism sounds crazy. But then, so did the idea of a heliocentric universe for many people, when Copernicus removed the earth from its privileged position in the universe. What seems counter-intuitive might just be true. And Berkeley always claimed that his immaterialist philosophy was commonsense.

THE WORLD IS JUST AS WE PERCEIVE IT TO BE.

IF ALL WE EVER PERCEIVE ARE IDEAS, AND WE HAVE NO REAL KNOWLEDGE OF MYSTERIOUS "MATERIAL SUBSTANCES" OR MATTER, WE MIGHT AS WELL DUMP THE ONE SUPERFLUOUS TERM THAT HAS NO USEFUL FUNCTION.

We may only perceive ideas but ideas don't just float around independently. They only exist when they are being *perceived*. So for anything to exist, it has to be perceived. Berkeley is therefore closely associated with the slogan "Esse est Percipi" – to exist is to be perceived.

A New Theory of Vision

Berkeley at first applied his immaterialist views solely to vision. We only ever *see* ideas, but (rather oddly) our sense of touch somehow does make contact with a real physical world. When we look at a landscape, we don't actually "see" distance, just a flat visual field which we soon learn, from moving around and from our sense of touch, has distance.

THE SAME IS TRUE OF SIZE. WE ALWAYS INTERPRET SIZE, WE NEVER SEE IT DIRECTLY, WHICH SUGGESTS THAT ALL OUR VISUAL EXPERIENCES ARE "IN THE MIND".

THE ONLY RELIABLE CONTACT WE HAVE WITH THE WORLD IS OUR SENSE OF TOUCH.

Our sense of sight and our sense of touch must be radically and wholly different. That is why a blind man with restored sight would have no chance of recognizing those objects he knew only through touch.
However, by the time Berkeley wrote *The Principles*, he had decided that we had no way of making any direct contact with the external world through our senses – not even through touch.

Abstract Ideas

Berkeley begins *The Principles* with an attack on Locke's doctrine of abstract ideas. Locke's doctrine of abstraction is malicious because it gives existence to entities that are unreal. Abstraction is the cause of numerous philosophical errors.

IT IS IMPOSSIBLE TO ABSTRACT THE IDEA OF "WHITE" FROM SEVERAL CONCRETE INSTANCES AND THEN ENTERTAIN A GENERAL IDEA OF PURE "WHITENESS" IN THE MIND.

THE IDEA WILL ALWAYS BE CONTAMINATED BY OTHER ELEMENTS OF SHAPE, SIZE OR LOCATION.

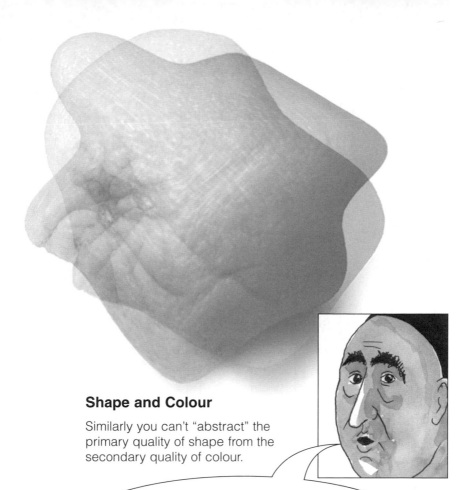

Shape and Colour

Similarly you can't "abstract" the primary quality of shape from the secondary quality of colour.

A COLOURLESS ORANGE IS NOT ONLY INCONCEIVABLE BUT WOULD HAVE NO VISIBLE "SHAPE". SHAPE AND COLOUR CANNOT BE SEPARATED. BOTH MUST BE SUBJECTIVE.

(Berkeley's philosophy is notorious for this type of conflated argument – you state something "obvious" and follow it with something more debatable in the hope that it will become acceptable by default.)

Most importantly of all, Locke's doctrine of "material substance" is an unimaginable abstraction. No one has ever experienced such a thing. In what sense is it "material" and how does it act as a "substratum" to "support" properties?

Triangles

Abstraction encourages philosophers to futile metaphysical debates. Berkeley insisted that only words and concepts whose ultimate origins lie in sense experience can have any meaning. Locke needed abstraction and general ideas in order to explain how it is that general words have meaning (by referring to general ideas in the mind). The abstract idea of the triangle gave the general word "triangle" its meaning.

No one can have a mental image of some weird "abstract triangle" that stands for all sorts of triangle.

3 STRAIGHT SIDES
AB, BC, CA
ANGLES TOTAL 180°

ONLY THAT WHICH IS *CONCEIVABLE* CAN MAKE SENSE. MY CONCEIVING OR IMAGINING POWER DOES NOT EXTEND BEYOND THE POSSIBILITY OF REAL EXISTENCE OR PERCEPTION.

Nevertheless, Berkeley cannot deny the existence or necessity of general words. So how do they work, if there are no "general ideas" for them to refer to?

Images of Particulars

His answer is that general words get their meaning by referring to one particular triangle which then "represents" all the others. For Berkeley, ideas are almost exclusively visual images in the mind, and those images must always be of particulars.

WHEN I TALK ABOUT "MAN", THE IMAGE IN MY MIND IS OF A SPECIFIC INDIVIDUAL WHO "STANDS FOR", OR "SIGNIFIES", ALL MEN.

This is because all we ever experience are individuals, not abstractions. This representation is usually also quite imprecise, which is why, of course, it works.

Language

Berkeley at first thought that words get their meaning from use, a very 20th-century explanation, but then he slipped back into the more familiar kind of 17th-century "ideational" theory.

He agreed with Locke that words get their meaning from referring to ideas in the mind, even if those ideas do not have to be continually present in our mind when we are speaking or listening to someone.

Words which are not anchored to ideas in this way are mostly without meaning. "Unattached" language is therefore remarkably treacherous. It leads to all sorts of confusions, usually caused by abstraction.

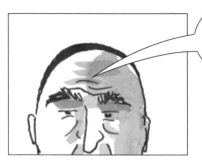

IT FOSSILIZES OUTDATED SCIENTIFIC THEORIES AND ENDOWS RECEIVED OPINIONS WITH AUTHORITY.

Hence, we still misleadingly talk about "sunrise", when presumably we should talk about "earthfall".

Similarly, the word "cat" is no more than the name we give to recurring patterns or "clusters" of sense experiences like shape, size, colour, movement, furry texture, musty smell and purring sounds.

How It All Works

Berkeley's philosophy is about perception, but is, inevitably, also an ontological and metaphysical theory about "what is real" and "what is fundamental". When we have sensory ideas, they do not flood into our minds in a random set of constantly changing shapes, colours and movements. They form an orderly series and group into "families". That's how our experiences make sense.

WE SEE A CAT-SHAPE IDEA AND WE STROKE A CAT-FUR IDEA, AND THE TWO EXPERIENCES CORRELATE.

This is a very convenient arrangement which has undoubtedly pushed human beings into believing in the existence of physical objects.

Everyday language is also very persuasive. Because we use the word "cat", we assume there is one physical object that matches up to the word. But all that exists are interrelated "bundles" of sensory experiences.

Dr Johnson's Refutation

Just because these sensory ideas are wholly cerebral doesn't make them anything like hallucinations or dreams. Sensory ideas are strong, clear, reliable and involuntary, whereas imaginary ideas are usually unpredictable and "unattached" to family groups.

I REFUTE YOUR DOCTRINE THUS!

DR JOHNSON THOUGHT THAT BY KICKING A STONE HE HAD REFUTED MY DOCTRINE. OF COURSE, ALL HE DID WAS TO CONFIRM IT.

HIS STONE EXPERIENCES CAME IN A BUNDLE AND INCLUDED THE TACTILE AS WELL AS THE VISUAL IDEA.

Samuel Johnson (1709–84), in fact, was a true convert, because Berkeley always insisted that, of all the sensory experiences in any one family, touch is always the most reliable. Our sensory experiences are also usually predictable and consistent. If we start to run water into a bath, and leave the bathroom for five minutes (which then ceases to exist, remember – existence and perception are the same), then, on our return, our sense experience is of a fuller bath than before.

Berkeley's Monist Argument

Berkeley thinks that ideas can only be entertained by minds, so all talk of external substances "supporting" ideas is unprovable. We can never show how our ideas are "copies" of anything.

NOR CAN WE EXPERIENCE OBJECTS OUTSIDE OF OUR IMMEDIATE PERCEPTION ...

WE HAVE NO LOGICAL WAY OF PROVING THAT OBJECTS IN THE ROOM NEXT DOOR EXIST UNPERCEIVED.

Imagination and Truth

Because Berkeley is committed to the notion of thinking as "seeing ideas", he's often persuaded by the "imagination argument" which suggests that perceiving and imagining are almost identical.

WE CANNOT IMAGINE PHYSICAL OBJECTS EXISTING INDEPENDENTLY FROM OUR THINKING ABOUT THEM.

SO THEY DO NOT.

We cannot imagine something that consists entirely of primary qualities. A shape can only be distinguished if it is coloured. Shape must therefore be as subjective as colour. We cannot conceive of "matter" at all, because we have had no experience of it. And so on.

But what I can or cannot imagine may have little to do with what is the case. Just because I cannot imagine or conceive of life on other planets does not mean that, logically, it cannot exist. Berkeley also explains why it is that the word "exists" means the same as "is perceived". It's not possible to talk meaningfully about the idea of something existing that is not being perceived. It's not possible to *think* that way.

AS SOON AS YOU THINK ABOUT AN UNPERCEIVED TREE, THERE YOU ARE, PERCEIVING IT, IN YOUR IMAGINATION.

So experiences cannot exist unexperienced.

Purely Mental Existence

Locke claimed that physical objects had objective "powers" to produce subjective sensations of secondary qualities in the mind. Berkeley ignores the objective status of these causative "powers" and insists that secondary qualities exist only in the mind. Water can feel hot to one hand and cold to another, so there is no such thing as objective temperature. It is wholly mind-dependent. Primary qualities are also relative and subjective.

BUT NO ONE BELIEVES THAT PAIN EXISTS OUTSIDE OF THE MIND, SO NEITHER CAN HEAT NOR THE FIRE ITSELF.

MY "TREE EXPERIENCES" ARE "BIG", BUT ONLY TO ME. THEIR SIZE, AND EXISTENCE, CANNOT BE SOMETHING APART FROM MY PERCEPTIONS.

A MAN WHO STANDS TOO CLOSE TO A FIRE WILL SOON FEEL HEAT, AND THEN PAIN.

The conclusion any rational person must come to is that only *mental phenomena* exist – that is, minds (or souls or "spirits") and ideas. But if material bodies cannot produce these ideas, and they do not originate from us, then they must originate from another mind that somehow forces them onto us. This immensely powerful mind belongs to God.

The Argument from God

We can infer that God exists, even if we do not directly experience Him, because there has to be a non-material cause of our ideas. Fortunately, God is good, which explains why He provides our finite human minds with orderly sense experiences. He directly plants sensory ideas into our minds which are vivid, consistent and coherent.

God also maintains sensory ideas for us to have when they are not being directly perceived. It seems that unperceived ideas do have a sort of existence after all.

Experiences awaiting perception

TREES
BALLS
GRASS

SENSE EXPERIENCES

GOD IS ABSOLUTELY ESSENTIAL TO THE WAY THINGS ARE.

(A theory of perception which almost makes Berkeley a "phenomenalist", of which more later.)

69

The Existence of the Self

Berkeley also insisted that we know that "minds" exist as well as ideas, because we have a "notion" of what mind is, if not a very clear mental image.

It is very difficult for a mind to inspect itself. We are never very sure about what would actually count as an idea of the mind.

The obvious problem for Berkeley's radical empiricism is that we have no direct immediate experiences of selves, minds or souls. He has to resort to the Cartesian solution: it is impossible to talk about perceiving ideas, unless there is a *perceiver*.

We may lack a clear idea of the soul, but we have a "notion" of one. And because, as Socrates said, the soul cannot be divided into parts, therefore it must be immortal. Berkeley's arguments for the existence of the self are rather weak and derivative, but then, the subject of minds is never one philosophers have found easy.

Science Depends on God

God's existence is also essential for science. Scientific understanding is possible because God makes our ideas regular and reliable. Berkeley thought that scientific investigation was still feasible, even though it could only ever be about *ideas* and not matter. His views were "instrumentalist": science is useful (but not necessarily true) because it can predict the regularities of sensory experiences. Scientific theories can reveal links between different ideas but never penetrate deeper realities. Newton had maintained that Time and Space were both "absolute" because neither depended on the existence of physical objects or our ideas of them.

TIME FLOWS EQUABLY, WITHOUT RELATION TO ANYTHING EXTERNAL.

I DISAGREE. "TIME" IS WHOLLY RELATIVE – MERELY THE SUCCESSION OF IDEAS IN OUR TEMPORAL MINDS, WITH NO OTHER SORT OF OBJECTIVE EXISTENCE.

Those who think about "Time" in Newton's absolutist way are victims of the heinous habit of abstraction. When no one is thinking, "time" ceases to exist.

71

Space and Numbers

Similarly, to talk about "Space" in Newton's absolute sense is really only valid when one is referring to spatial relations as they exist in the mind. Berkeley also claimed that numbers cannot exist somehow outside of a mind doing mathematics.

Mathematics is something we invent. This is a view which makes Berkeley a "Formalist", someone who believes numbers are useful fictions without independent reality. Berkeley's philosophy of science now seems rather modern. **Werner Heisenberg**'s (1901–76) concept of the Uncertainty Principle in quantum theory emphasizes the role of the observer's "interference" that can affect experimentation in sub-particle physics. Space and Time are probably more Berkelean than Newtonian, if **Albert Einstein**'s (1879–1955) relativity theories remain correct.

God and Minds

All that exists is One Infinite Mind and our millions of finite ones – one continually transmitting ideas and the others continually receiving them. That's all there is.

WE DON'T SIT ON CHAIRS, BUT ON BUNDLES OF IDEAS. WHEN WE CLOSE OUR EYES, THINGS CEASE TO EXIST.

THE BED IN THE ROOM NEXT DOOR DOES NOT EXIST BECAUSE, AT PRESENT, IT IS UNPERCEIVED. YET SOMEHOW IT EXISTS IN GOD'S MIND AS A BUNDLE OF IDEAS WAITING THERE TO BE PERCEIVED.

It's a philosophical account of perception and reality that seems "utterly absurd and utterly irrefutable".

Is Berkeley Irrefutable?

Berkeley's philosophy appears to be "irrefutable" because we cannot prove that unperceived objects exist from observation. We can only suppose or infer that they do. We cannot prove they do through any process of induction because we have no previous observational opportunities to rely on. We cannot deduce that they exist, because we have no premises to work with.

I WIN THE ARGUMENT!

But not many of us are persuaded that Berkeley's conclusions are true.

Are the Arguments Convincing?

Berkeley claimed that since his philosophy was a beautifully simple account of perception, minds, reality and knowledge, it must likely be true. Idealism relieves us of worries about "substance", how it is that matter can think, or what "reality" is "really like". But it does make massive demands on our natural ways of thinking about ourselves and the world. To become true Berkeleans requires a "paradigm shift" away from all our deeply embedded belief systems.

Berkeley assails us with a barrage of clever arguments that most of us can recognize as strange or invalid, although it is often hard to see why they are.

ONCE YOU ACKNOWLEDGE, SAY, THAT PAIN IS IN THE MIND, AND HEAT CAUSES PAIN, THEN YOU ARE ON THE SLIPPERY SLOPE TO BERKELEY'S IDEALISM.

GETTING OFF DEMANDS A CLEAR DISTINCTION BETWEEN THE ACT OF *FEELING* HEAT AND THE HEAT OF THE FIRE THAT *CAUSED* IT.

Begging the Question

Berkeley's arguments are traps that "beg the question". They use what he wants to prove as proof. If you agree with him from the start that physical objects are merely ideas, then it's very easy to confuse the following two propositions.

> No one can think of physical objects existing without a mind to do so.

> No one can think of physical objects existing outside of mind.

It's clear that we cannot imagine thoughts without a mind to think them. But this doesn't prohibit us from thinking about physical objects existing *outside* of minds.

I PERSONALLY REMAIN CONFIDENT THAT ALL THE CONTENTS OF THE BEDROOM NEXT DOOR ARE STILL QUITE HAPPILY EXISTING, EVEN THOUGH THEY ARE PRESENTLY UNPERCEIVED ...

... BUT I CANNOT PROVE IT.

God's Intervention

When I leave the tap running, and return to my "unperceived" bathroom, isn't it more likely that the tap has been running in my absence, than that God has intervened with some kind of ingenious conjuring trick? As soon as Berkeley brings God into his Immaterialism, it becomes much less convincing.

And if our sense experiences are all that we ever know, how do we know that other people exist with minds of their own, and are not equally figments of God's imagination? Berkeley's Idealism can easily lead to a kind of solipsistic madness.

PERHAPS THERE ARE MILLIONS OF INDIVIDUALS ALL HYPNOTIZED INTO HAVING SENSORY EXPERIENCES OF EACH OTHER?

And if all we ever experience are immediate sensory ideas, how can we be confident that it is indeed God who is the cause of them? No one has a sense experience of God, and yet Berkeley still demands that we believe in **His** existence, but **not** in the more humdrum existence of everyday physical objects.

The Counter-argument from Evolution

It would seem more rational for God to create matter and let that be the cause of our ideas. This might be why He gave us rather elaborate organs of perception.

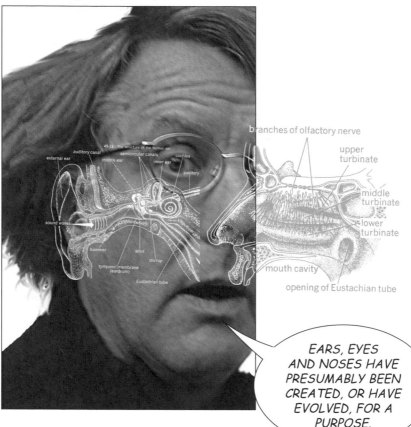

EARS, EYES AND NOSES HAVE PRESUMABLY BEEN CREATED, OR HAVE EVOLVED, FOR A PURPOSE.

Fortunately, Berkeley never had to reconcile Immaterialism with evolutionary theory. But there is no doubt that he would have produced some ingenious explanation to incorporate it into his doctrine. So, philosophers sometimes get irritated with Berkeley's methods because they can appear more like clever tricks of paradox rather than a genuine search for what is true.

David Hume

David Hume (1711–76) was born in Edinburgh and died there. His parents were affluent members of the Scottish landed gentry. As a student at Edinburgh University he was taught Locke's philosophy and became acquainted with Berkeley's. He was living in France when he wrote his first book, *A Treatise of Human Nature* (1740), which was not well received.

UNDAUNTED, I SUBSEQUENTLY WROTE A MORE ACCESSIBLE VERSION OF THE SAME PHILOSOPHY IN AN ENQUIRY CONCERNING HUMAN UNDERSTANDING (1748).

During his own lifetime he was famous as a historian and infamous as a notorious atheist. He spent the latter years of his life as a tutor to several children of the French aristocracy, as a librarian, as a secretary to the English Ambassador to France, and as a civil servant.

Hume's Philosophy of Scepticism

Hume converted empiricism into a sceptical philosophy that would have shocked Berkeley. He attacked Christian belief in miracles and denied that God's existence could ever be proved. He showed that the foundations of science are deeply metaphysical and far more uncertain than anyone ever realized.

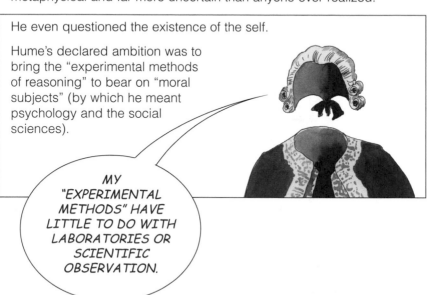

He even questioned the existence of the self.

Hume's declared ambition was to bring the "experimental methods of reasoning" to bear on "moral subjects" (by which he meant psychology and the social sciences).

MY "EXPERIMENTAL METHODS" HAVE LITTLE TO DO WITH LABORATORIES OR SCIENTIFIC OBSERVATION.

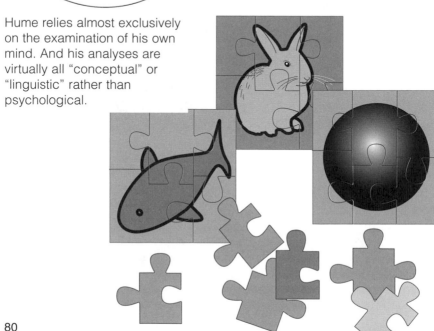

Hume relies almost exclusively on the examination of his own mind. And his analyses are virtually all "conceptual" or "linguistic" rather than psychological.

Ideas and Impressions

Hume's philosophy tries to avoid all the confusions caused by the ambiguities of that "idea" word. The Humean mind has access to both "impressions" and ideas. "Impressions" are forceful and clear, they "impress" themselves onto the mind, whereas "ideas" are fainter – as befits copies of originals. Most impressions are derived from perception, but some originate from reflection – when they are accompanied by strong feelings of pain or pleasure.

IDEA   IMPRESSION

THE "IDEA" OF BEING IN LOVE MAKES NOTHING LIKE THE FORCEFUL IMPRESSION ...

... OF ACTUALLY BEING IN LOVE.

Hume agrees with Locke on how knowledge gradually accumulates. The mind endlessly assembles impressions (which are involuntary and indivisible) into simple and complex ideas.

Impressions and Truth

Original impressions inevitably place restrictions on those ideas we can subsequently imagine. For instance, the complex idea of a mermaid is based on two impressions – that of a woman and that of a fish.

The idea of God is based on original impressions of human wisdom and intelligence, exaggerated. This is how and why Hume arrives at his most important philosophical doctrine.

THERE CAN BE NO SIMPLE "IDEA" WITHOUT A CORRESPONDING "IMPRESSION".

Hume often employs this doctrine as a kind of verification procedure, to test for truth and meaning. If you can track an idea back to some original impression, then it probably makes some kind of sense. If you can't, then the idea is probably nonsense.

The Criteria of Force and Vivacity

Hume's doctrine of impressions is vital to his whole empiricist doctrine. Impressions can only be distinguished from ideas psychologically, because of their perceived clarity and ebullience. This inevitably produces problems. Can we always distinguish an impression from an idea?

MEMORIES

BELIEFS

I MAINTAIN THAT WE RECOGNIZE MEMORIES AND BELIEFS (OUR IMPRESSIONS) BECAUSE BOTH ARE MORE "FORCEFUL" THAN MERE IMAGININGS (IDEAS).

IMAGININGS

But sometimes our imaginings can be far more vivid than distant memories. So the distinction between impression and idea isn't perfectly convincing. Nor does Hume examine the crucial relationship between *belief* and *knowledge* in much depth. This is partly because he thinks that human beings are habitual and indiscriminate believers, but, in reality, **know** very little indeed.

The External World

Hume understood the philosophy of Locke and admired some of Berkeley's work. But whether he was a representative realist or a full-blooded idealist is difficult to ascertain. He seems to have remained happily agnostic about the existence of an "external" world and says surprisingly little about it.

ALL THAT WE CAN BE SURE OF IS THE EXISTENCE OF IMPRESSIONS.

He rehearses all the familiar objections to any belief in the existence of matter. We cannot bypass the impressions provided by our senses in order to find out whether they are true copies of "originals". Nor can we prove any logical connection between physical objects and our impressions. So physical objects may not be the cause of our sensory experiences.

Philosophy and Everyday Life

Fortunately, our impressions are mostly coherent and constant, a factor which inevitably pushes us into believing in the existence of an external world.

IT SEEMS TO ME PSYCHOLOGICALLY IMPOSSIBLE FOR HUMAN BEINGS TO LIVE THEIR DAILY LIVES DOUBTING THAT PHYSICAL OBJECTS EXIST.

BUT THAT DOES NOT MEAN THEIR BELIEF IS JUSTIFIED.

The existence of "things out there" is just not the central issue of Hume's philosophy. The primary focus is on what happens in the mind, and how we can analyse its contents.

Hume's Fork

Hume classified all philosophical statements, propositions or "truth claims" into two kinds: *matters of fact* and *relations of ideas*.

A statement like **"A triangle is a three-sided figure"** depends entirely on the relationship of the ideas it contains, and is provable by "the mere operation of thought" or conceptual analysis.

The truth of a proposition like **"Smith is male"** depends on a fact being claimed about the world and is only verifiable by observation.

MATTERS OF FACT

RELATIONS OF IDEAS

MY "FORK" SAYS THAT **ALL** KNOWLEDGE "FORKS" INTO THESE TWO KINDS - TRUTHS OF REASON AND TRUTHS OF FACT.

KNOWLEDGE

This is a very important distinction which helped to clear up all kinds of philosophical muddles, notably the problem of "causation". (Hume insisted causation was a matter of fact, not a logical necessity.)

Science, Theology and Proof

Ever since Plato, philosophers have always admired "relations of ideas" because there is a reassuring "necessity" or guaranteed certainty about them.

2+2 **has** to equal 4.

All bachelors **have** to be unmarried.

MATTERS OF FACT

RELATIONS OF IDEAS

> MATTERS OF FACT NEVER HAVE THAT KIND OF CERTAINTY BECAUSE THE WORLD ISN'T ALWAYS RELIABLE. SMITH MAY BE FEMALE.

What Hume's distinction means is that all claims to existence, all problems of causation, and all science can never be like the truths of maths and logic beyond all possible doubt. There can be no "demonstrative science" and no way that God's existence can be definitively proved. Furthermore, if statements seem to be neither relations of ideas nor matters of fact (like a lot of theology), then they are probably nonsense masquerading as sense.

THEOLOGY

FACT

REASON

The Problem of Cause and Effect

Until Hume, philosophers and theologians normally assumed that "cause and effect" were as reliable as logical necessity. Everything **must** have a cause, just as 2+2 **must** be 4. Theologians believed it must be possible to prove God's existence definitively as the "first cause" of all subsequent causes and effects.

If every event "must" have a cause, then, going back in time, there "must" have been one **uncaused** initial cause (God) who started off the causal chain. So God's existence is proved.

FIRE CAUSES SMOKE, MOSQUITO BITES CAUSE MALARIA, SMOKING CAUSES CANCER. BUT WHAT *IS* CAUSE ITSELF?

What is Cause?

Hume's conceptual analysis of cause goes like this ...

Cause cannot be **a priori** (purely a matter of thinking) like mathematics and logic.

If it were, we would always know what effects would result from each and every cause.

BUT WE DON'T.

So it must (according to Hume's Fork) be an empirical problem, a "matter of fact". Let's look more closely into this "matter of fact" of cause and effect ...

The Appearance of Constant Conjunction

We can see that cause involves effect in "constant conjunction". Whenever there is one, there is the other.

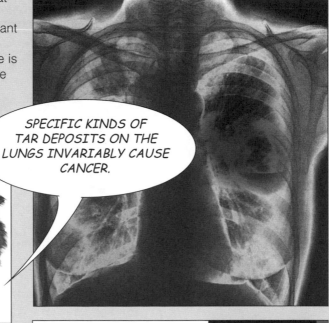

We can see that cause always includes *temporal priority*. An effect never precedes a cause. There is no "backward causation".

What is Necessity?

So far, so good. But can we see the "necessary" part of cause? None of us can accept that, one day, there might be "a causeless event". But can we see the "mustness" of causation? Or "cause itself"? What exactly are we talking about?

The obvious problem for empiricists is that you cannot "see" cause. It is an idea without any corresponding impression. You can see the conjunction when one billiard ball hits another – the first has to move before the other can – but you cannot see "the causal necessity".

WE ONLY FIND THAT THE ONE DOES, IN FACT ...

... FOLLOW THE OTHER.

In Humean language, there is no original impression for this idea of "necessity" and, just as damning, we have absolutely no idea of the sort of phenomenon we would be looking for. So why do we think that cause is "necessary"?

Cause is Psychological and not Logical

WHY ARE WE SO CERTAIN? IF MY MOTORBIKE MECHANIC SAID, AS HE OFTEN DOES ...

I CANNOT SEE WHAT THE CAUSE IS FOR THIS ENGINE FAILURE.

I MIGHT ACCEPT WHAT HE SAYS BUT TELL HIM TO GO ON LOOKING.

BUT IF HE THEN SAID ....

THE ENGINE WILL NOT WORK, AND THERE IS NO CAUSE FOR ITS MALFUNCTION.

I JUST COULDN'T ACCEPT IT, ALTHOUGH I'M NOT REALLY CLEAR WHY. DOES THERE *HAVE* TO BE A CAUSE, OR DO I JUST *BELIEVE* THERE HAS TO BE?

Hume Explains "Why"

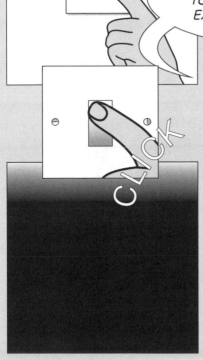

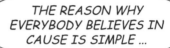

THE REASON WHY EVERYBODY BELIEVES IN CAUSE IS SIMPLE ...

Causal "necessity" is psychological, not logical. All we ever observe are constant conjunctions in the world, not causes, and we acquire a "disposition" to expect Bs when we see As, or vice versa. We expect there to be smoke when we see fire and vice versa. It's a very sensible expectation, based on experience, but that's all there is to it.

... CAUSE IS JUST A GENERALIZATION THAT WE COME TO, BASED ON OUR NUMEROUS EXPERIENCES OF THE WORLD.

Eventually it gets ingrained into our minds. But there is nothing intrinsically causal about the world, or, if there is, then it comes with no guarantee. So the "cosmological" or "causal" argument for God's existence is misconceived. After Hume's analysis, no one ever talked about cause in the same way again, or with the same degree of confidence.

93

Induction and Deduction

Induction and causation are linked. Induction is simply the process of looking at the world and using our observations to come to general conclusions about it. Induction has many uses, one of which is predicting the future.

BLACKBIRDS CAN "FORESEE THE FUTURE". THEY RETURN TO MY BIRD TABLE TODAY BECAUSE THERE WAS SOGGY BREAD THERE YESTERDAY.

I assume that the sun will rise above the horizon tomorrow morning because it has done so lots of times. But, like causation, induction is a "matter of fact", and so can never be absolutely certain, unlike deductive logic.

Rules of Deductive Logic

One reason why deductive logic "works" is because of the "conclusion and premise rule". A conclusion cannot contain more information than is already in the premises.

All men have lungs
This is a man
Therefore he has lungs

DEDUCTIVE LOGIC IS ESSENTIALLY AN EMPTY TRICK WHICH "WORKS" BECAUSE IT MERELY REPEATS WHAT IS ALREADY IMPLICIT, IF NOT BLINDINGLY OBVIOUS.

All men have lungs
This is a man
Therefore **he can breathe**

BUT WE OFTEN JUMP TO CONCLUSIONS ...

This time the conclusion is invalid. Where is breathing mentioned in the two premises? Induction sometimes looks like it's doing the same sort of logical trick, but it isn't.

All men I have observed **so far** have lungs
Therefore, **all** men have lungs

It's a very strong possibility that all living men do have lungs, but this argument does not prove it. The conclusion "jumps" from a limited set of observations (some men) to a universal truth (all men).

THIS INDUCTIVE CONCLUSION CLEARLY ISN'T DEDUCTIVELY VALID.

The Uses of Induction

It is impossible to make induction deductive, however reliable it appears to be. This is because it is based on observations of the world, a place which is normally reliable but can surprise.

I MAY FORGET TO PUT BREAD OUT,

THE EARTH MAY GET NUDGED AWAY FROM ITS ORBIT,

ONE DAY A MAN MAY BREATHE THROUGH ARTIFICIAL GILLS.

So inductive "reasoning" cannot be made into a relation of ideas. But neither are its conclusions empirically verifiable. (No one can observe an infinite number of men, now and in the future.) All we can do is accept that induction produces useful information about probabilities. It is probable that all men have lungs, that my local blackbirds will eat, that the sun will rise. Just as we are habituated by repetition to believe in causation, so we are with induction. It is "an animal impulse" or instinct which we cannot evade.

Solutions to the Problem

Hume thought the "problem" of induction was inherently insoluble. It is only a problem if you assume that induction is deduction. Some philosophers argue that Hume is misusing language when he claims that we do not truly "know" what induction tells us.

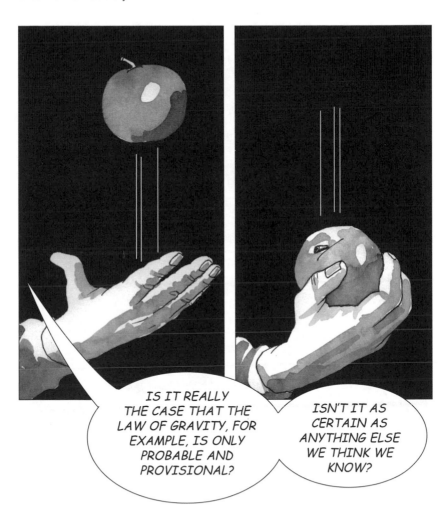

IS IT REALLY THE CASE THAT THE LAW OF GRAVITY, FOR EXAMPLE, IS ONLY PROBABLE AND PROVISIONAL?

ISN'T IT AS CERTAIN AS ANYTHING ELSE WE THINK WE KNOW?

Hume's definition of "knowledge" seems absurdly narrow, when he suggests that we can only ever "know" the conclusions of logic and mathematics.

The Response of Pragmatism

Pragmatists welcome induction because it has shown itself to be extremely useful (so far!). Deduction only works because of its timidity. Its conclusions never "tell you more". The whole point of induction, on the other hand, is its ability to tell you extra about the probabilities involving all men, all sunrises, all days in the future.

We're stuck with it. There is no other method of prediction we can use to make life intelligible. Nevertheless, what Hume shows us is that there are very few things we know for sure.

What About Identity?

Human identity presents an obvious problem for empiricists. We can never have direct *sensory* experiences of mind, soul or personality, except perhaps through introspection. Both Locke and Berkeley argued that there had to be some kind of entity perceiving ideas. But in *The Treatise*, Hume famously suggested that there is no such thing as a human self. Again, he relies on his "impression/idea" test. We may have an idea of mind, but where is the impression to back it up?

HOWEVER MUCH WE LOOK INTO OURSELVES, WE FAIL TO FIND SOME IMPRESSION FOR OUR IDEA OF "MIND".

So, rather oddly, the organ that has impressions and is the "owner" of them, does not produce an impression of itself.

Looking Within

All we ever perceive introspectively are bundles of ideas, but never something that might count as "mental substance". The self is either a hypothetical entity, based on inference, a convenient and unexamined fiction, like that of "physical objects", or, more oddly, a kind of process.

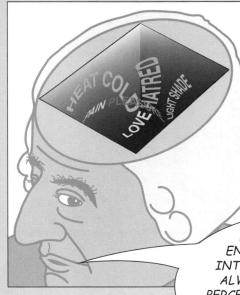

FOR MY PART, WHEN I ENTER MOST INTIMATELY INTO WHAT I CALL MYSELF, I ALWAYS STUMBLE ON SOME PERCEPTION OR OTHER, OF HEAT OR COLD, LIGHT OR SHADE, LOVE OR HATRED, PAIN OR PLEASURE.

I NEVER CATCH MYSELF AT ANY TIME WITHOUT A PERCEPTION, AND NEVER CAN OBSERVE ANYTHING BUT THE PERCEPTION.

This means that when perceptions cease, so does the self. For Hume, there is no immortal soul. But what would actually count as an "impression" of the mind or self remains unclear. Hume's radical scepticism does not impede him from using personal pronouns like "I", or referring to "my" impressions, "my" sensations and so on. Human identity was a problem that Hume finally confessed was "too hard for my understanding".

Hume on Free Will

One problem that has always worried philosophers is "free will". If all events are "determined" by cause, perhaps all our own choices and decisions are also. This means that none of us is ever truly "free", even though we think we are. Hume's way out of this dilemma was partly to dismiss the belief in the "necessity" of causation. Causes and effects are, after all, not indissolubly linked by some iron-like necessity, but are wholly psychological.

SO THERE IS NO "NECESSITY" ABOUT HUMAN ACTIONS. HUMAN BEINGS REMAIN FREE, BECAUSE THEY THEMSELVES ARE THE "CAUSE" OF THEIR ACTIONS.

Religion, Proof and Design

Hume was an atheist. He argued that miracles were improbable because there was very little evidence to show they had occurred. What is more probable – that "miracles" actually happen or that those who witness them are either credulous, mistaken or lying? One proof of God's existence is the "teleological" proof, or the argument from the "design" that we see in the world. The universe looks like a complex and well-designed machine, so it *must* have a designer.

Just because the world looks ordered, this doesn't mean that it must have had a designer. To make inductive inferences about "design" we also need more than one example – but in this instance we have only one universe. The universe might have had *several* designers. Human beings are always happy to assume that the universe has been created for their convenience.

But we, and the universe, are just as likely to be products of chance.

Immanuel Kant (1724–1804) subsequently suggested that it is we humans who impose "design" onto the universe. "Design" is not something we observe.

THE UNIVERSE MAY BE LESS ORDERED THAN WAS ONCE SUPPOSED.

HAD HUME BENEFITED FROM KNOWLEDGE OF EVOLUTIONARY THEORY OR QUANTUM PHYSICS, THEN HIS CRITICISM OF THE TELEOLOGICAL ARGUMENT WOULD HAVE GONE FURTHER.

Ethics, Moral Language and Fact

Hume revolutionized ethics, or more accurately, our understanding of the meanings we assign to moral language. His main point is that moral language is not factual but evaluative. When I say "War is evil", I may think that I am describing war objectively, whereas I am only telling you about my subjective feelings. No one can empirically detect the "evil" of war. Such an entity produces no *impressions* on the mind. (Unlike, say, the more factual "War is destructive of life and property.")

"WAR IS EVIL" SEEMS TO MEAN LITTLE MORE THAN "I DISLIKE WAR".

If his analysis is correct, this means that it is impossible for anyone to "prove" their moral beliefs or feelings, no matter how much factual evidence they can muster.

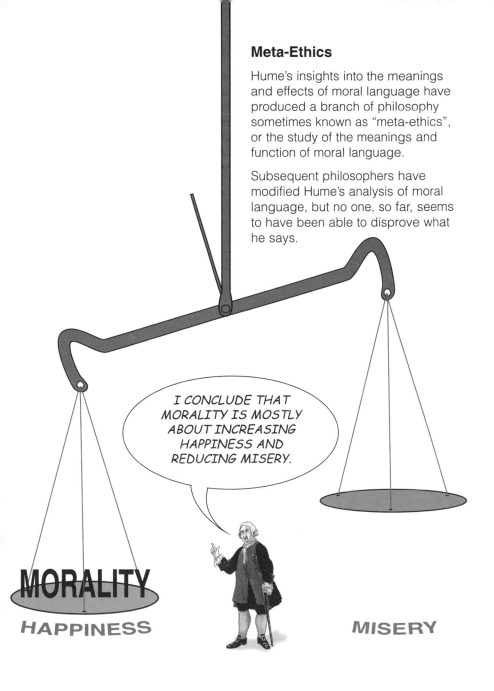

Meta-Ethics

Hume's insights into the meanings and effects of moral language have produced a branch of philosophy sometimes known as "meta-ethics", or the study of the meanings and function of moral language.

Subsequent philosophers have modified Hume's analysis of moral language, but no one, so far, seems to have been able to disprove what he says.

I CONCLUDE THAT MORALITY IS MOSTLY ABOUT INCREASING HAPPINESS AND REDUCING MISERY.

MORALITY

HAPPINESS

MISERY

A view that would be pursued with great enthusiasm and vigour by other philosophers in the following century – as we shall soon see ...

Conclusions on Hume

Hume used the tools of empiricism as a way of challenging nearly all our basic human beliefs. We actually *know* very little. Logic cannot "jump" from facts to moral conclusions. Induction cannot be made logical. Causation is in us, not out there, and there may be no "us" at all. Hume's doctrine of "impressions" and "ideas" quickly reveals that there is little empirical evidence for most of our ideas.

BUT IF HUMAN BEINGS ARE NO MORE THAN BUNDLES OF "IMPRESSIONS", AND THERE ARE NO PHYSICAL OBJECTS, THEN IMPRESSIONS MUST BE CRUCIAL AND RATHER PECULIAR.

THEY CANNOT BE EXCLUSIVELY PHYSICAL OR MENTAL EITHER.

THEY ARE "NEUTRAL" PHENOMENA, FROM WHICH ALL OUR MISTAKEN BELIEFS ABOUT MIND AND MATTER DERIVE.

But Hume is never clear about what impressions are or how they differ from ideas. They are an analytic and critical tool more than anything else.

Kant's Criticism of Hume

Hume's destructive analysis of many unthinkingly held human beliefs stimulated the German philosopher Immanuel Kant into defending them in his famous and notoriously difficult *Critique of Pure Reason* (1781). Kant's defence of knowledge is nevertheless "critical" and postulates the natural limits of reason.

HUME WAS LOOKING FOR "IMPRESSIONS" THAT COULD NOT POSSIBLY EXIST – BECAUSE THEY ARE INBUILT AND UNAVOIDABLE FEATURES OF THE HUMAN MIND.

WE SEE A WORLD FULL OF PHYSICAL OBJECTS CAUSING EVENTS AND EXISTING IN SPACE AND TIME, BECAUSE THAT IS HOW OUR BRAINS ARE "WIRED UP".

We don't inspect the world and get "habituated" by it but project concepts upon it. Perhaps it is we who make the world human, not the world that frames how we think. But that's the subject of another book altogether.

107

J.S. Mill's Empirical Philosophy

John Stuart Mill (1806–73) is the most important
English philosopher of the 19th century. His father,
James Mill (1773–1836), crammed his son with
knowledge almost as soon as he was born and
allowed him no childhood friends. Understandably,
when he was 21, he had a nervous breakdown.

I CURED MYSELF WITH LONG WALKS AND POETRY.

He worked as an employee of the East India
Company for many years and was a Member of
Parliament for a short time. His personal and
political life were greatly influenced by Mrs Harriet
Taylor, his eventual wife. His most famous works
are *A System of Logic* (1843), *On Liberty* (1859)
and *Utilitarianism* (1863). Mill was also a great
reformer who agitated for parliamentary reform
and women's rights. And he was a very radical
empiricist.

The Permanent Possibility of Sensation

Mill is usually thought of as the founder of "Phenomenalism". This doctrine insists that all that we are ever aware of is "phenomena" or appearances – not "noumena" or substances.

BALL, BRASS, HARD, SHINY, POLISHED, COLD, METALLIC, BALL

PUFFY COTTON COMFY WARM SOFT FEATHERS WHITE SMELL FABRIC

OUR KNOWLEDGE OF OBJECTS CONSISTS OF NOTHING BUT THE SENSATIONS WHICH THEY EXCITE, OR WHICH WE IMAGINE THEM EXCITING, IN OURSELVES.

BALL BRASS HARD SHINY POLISHED COLD METALLIC BALL

Phenomenalism differs from Idealism because it enables you to talk about possible as well as actual sense experiences. It does not matter much if something is actually being perceived or not, but whether or not it is perceivable in practice.

109

Possible Sensations

The problem of "unperceived objects" is thereby lessened, if not solved. Berkeley's God is no longer required to maintain that which human beings do not or cannot see. Mill is an orthodox empiricist in all the usual ways: sensations occur in fixed groups, but we have no evidence of any "substratum" or "hidden cause" for collections of ideas.

THE BED NEXT DOOR MIGHT NOT EXIST AS A PHYSICAL OBJECT - BUT WHAT DOES EXIST IS A SET OF COHERENT POTENTIAL EXPERIENCES, ACTIVATED WHENEVER I ENTER THE ROOM.

MATTER IS THE PERMANENT POSSIBILITY OF SENSATION.

When we talk about physical objects, we are really talking about "possible sensations". A simple statement like "There is a bed in the room next door" should be reconstructed as "If someone were in that room, then they would have bed-like experiences". It's a rather desperate solution to Berkeley's problem. Mill seems to be sometimes "reducing" physical objects to that which is more philosophically acceptable and sometimes trying to eliminate them altogether.

Why Do We Believe in Objects?

Representative realists, like Locke, think that physical objects must be the cause of our ideas. Phenomenalists like Mill think that we *construct* physical objects out of our sensations. But why do most of us still believe in them? Mill maintains that our belief in the existence of physical objects is not innate, or rational, but an "acquired disposition". Once we have experienced a group of sensations, our minds come to expect further identical or similar sensations.

WE TEND TO THINK OF THESE POTENTIAL "SIMILAR SENSATIONS" AS PERMANENT. THIS MAKES US ASSUME THAT THEY HAVE AN OBJECTIVE REAL EXISTENCE, SEPARATE FROM OUR PERCEPTIONS OF THEM.

The constant regularity of our experiences not only establishes ingrained expectations in our minds but also makes most perception spontaneous.

Problems with Mill's Position

But what kind of existence (or "ontological status") do "possible experiences" have? Mill thinks they are somehow objective, independent of us, and that we receive them involuntarily. But how can sensations "exist" independently of minds?

SOME PHILOSOPHERS THINK THAT PERHAPS THEY "SUBSIST" – IN THE WAY THAT PERHAPS NUMBERS AND CONCEPTS DO.

OTHERS SAY THAT WE SHOULD REALLY THINK OF "POSSIBLE EXPERIENCES" AS BEING SIMILAR TO EXPECTATIONS OR BELIEFS.

THIS IS NOT VERY CLEAR.

Mill's attempt to solve or dissolve the problem of the supposed existence of unperceived objects remains unconvincing.

Mathematics

Hume differentiated "relations of ideas" radically from empirical "matters of fact". We know that 2+2 must necessarily equal 4 without confirmation of experience. But Mill insisted that **all** our knowledge has to come from experience. His explanation therefore took the extremely radical approach that deductive knowledge, in mathematics and logic, is really *inductive*. Numbers are a "huge generalization" from all the objects we have observed.

From an early age we learn that two bricks and two bricks makes four bricks. From this we assume that similar assemblies of objects will produce the same results.

His startling conclusion is that mathematics is therefore not "necessary" but only probable, like all inductive generalizations.

IT'S NOT VERY LIKELY THAT ONE DAY, 2 AND 2 WILL MAKE 3, BUT IT REMAINS A POSSIBILITY.

Our minds cannot conceive of ever counting two chairs and two chairs, and finding they add up to three, but that is because we have never experienced such an event before, not because such a thing is logically impossible. Mill's explanation of how mathematics "works" still seems utterly implausible.

Mill's Logic

Mill maintained that the fundamental "rules" of logic are also derived from our observations of the world. (We know that a statement can be either true or false, but not both – because this is what the world teaches us.) And although deductive logic appears to produce knowledge that is guaranteed, Mill points out that it has a major weakness. The premises of deduction are always derived from observation and induction.

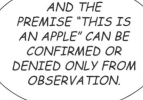

I CAN NEVER BE TOTALLY SURE THAT "GRAVITY MAKES ALL APPLES FALL" BECAUSE IT IS AN INDUCTIVE GENERALIZATION WHICH IS ONLY PROBABLE.

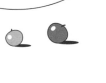

AND THE PREMISE "THIS IS AN APPLE" CAN BE CONFIRMED OR DENIED ONLY FROM OBSERVATION.

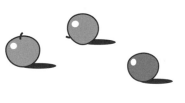

Induction

Hume showed that induction could only ever reach conclusions that are probable. Mill agreed that induction moves from "the known to the unknown", because the world is not always reliable or uniform.

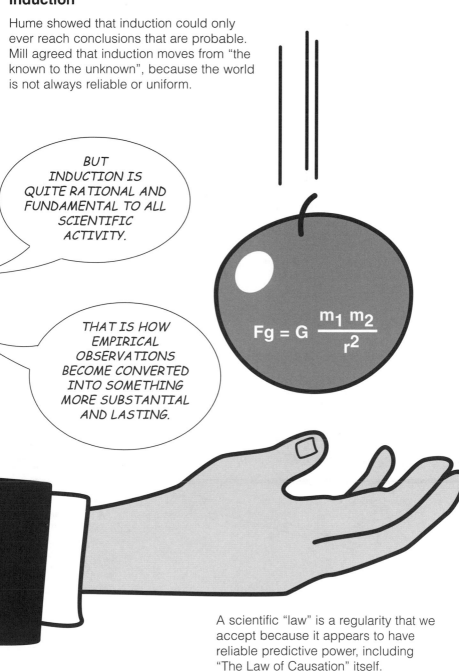

BUT INDUCTION IS QUITE RATIONAL AND FUNDAMENTAL TO ALL SCIENTIFIC ACTIVITY.

THAT IS HOW EMPIRICAL OBSERVATIONS BECOME CONVERTED INTO SOMETHING MORE SUBSTANTIAL AND LASTING.

$$Fg = G \frac{m_1 \, m_2}{r^2}$$

A scientific "law" is a regularity that we accept because it appears to have reliable predictive power, including "The Law of Causation" itself.

Mill's Treatment of Cause

Human experience has shown us that, so far, every event has always had a cause. But there is nothing logical or "necessary" about causation. Our knowledge of it is based on experience and induction. Causation means something like "all the conditions needed for an event to occur". "Necessary conditions" mean those which are vital for the event to happen. Many of these are obvious, others less so, because they are so fundamental.

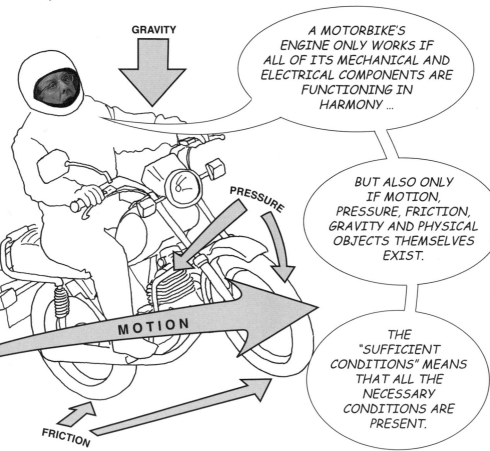

GRAVITY

A MOTORBIKE'S ENGINE ONLY WORKS IF ALL OF ITS MECHANICAL AND ELECTRICAL COMPONENTS ARE FUNCTIONING IN HARMONY ...

PRESSURE

BUT ALSO ONLY IF MOTION, PRESSURE, FRICTION, GRAVITY AND PHYSICAL OBJECTS THEMSELVES EXIST.

MOTION

THE "SUFFICIENT CONDITIONS" MEANS THAT ALL THE NECESSARY CONDITIONS ARE PRESENT.

FRICTION

If one necessary condition is absent (no petrol), then the conditions are not sufficient. In practice, of course, my motor mechanic tends not to worry overmuch about the existence of the material world, and usually singles out one or two more obvious necessary causes. But what we select and count as "the cause" often has more to do with what seems important to us at any one time, than with what is the most fundamental necessary cause.

What are Minds?

Mill was interested in how the mind learns and adapts to the world by continually associating ideas. But what is mind? Mill agrees with Hume that the mind is "nothing but the series of our sensations". We have no direct experience of minds. Both matter and minds are conjectural. But this neutrality about both "substances" can give rise to solipsism (that is, only my experiences exist, even my experiences of other people). Mill nevertheless argues that the existence of other minds is highly probable.

I RECOGNIZE THAT MY SENSATIONS OF OTHER HUMAN BEINGS HAVE MANY OBSERVABLE FEATURES IN COMMON WITH MYSELF.

SO IT IS PROBABLE THAT THEY ARE AS CONSCIOUS AS I AM.

Like Hume too, Mill finds it hard to explain why his own series of experiences feel unique. Human identity, consciousness and the concept of self seem to remain "inexplicable facts".

Mill's Ethics and Politics

Mill wrote extensively on the problems of perception and the philosophy of science. But he is most famous as a moral and political philosopher. The young Mill met and admired **Jeremy Bentham** (1748–1832), the founder of the ethical doctrine of Utilitarianism, and became wholly convinced by it.

Bentham genuinely believed that it was possible to make both morality and law "scientific".

THE FUNDAMENTAL EMPIRICAL TRUTH ABOUT THE PSYCHOLOGY AND PHYSIOLOGY OF HUMAN BEINGS IS THAT THEY PREFER PLEASURE TO PAIN.

IT IS THEREFORE THE MORAL DUTY OF INDIVIDUALS AND GOVERNMENTS TO MAXIMIZE HAPPINESS AND MINIMIZE PAIN.

Bentham believed that happiness could be measured in terms of its intensity, duration, reliability, and so on. Utilitarianism must also be democratic, since happiness must be distributed as widely as possible. Traditional moral rules are usually a good guide to moral judgements and behaviour, but they are not compulsory. (A mother with many starving children might be allowed to steal bread, if this produced more happiness than misery.)

PAIN

Higher Pleasures

Bentham's moral philosophy is methodical but not always very subtle. In *Utilitarianism* (1863), Mill attempted to redefine and defend it. He was concerned that "the tyranny of the majority" might inflict a general lowering of aesthetic taste. If the majority is happiest watching Reality TV, then programme-makers might exclusively provide such programmes. Mill's solution was to be mildly élitist.

HAPPINESS

READING WORDSWORTH IS STILL BETTER FOR YOU THAN PLAYING SKITTLES AND DRINKING ALE.

Mill insisted that high culture produces more permanent varieties of happiness and so should not be dispensed with entirely.

Bentham thought that the principles of Utility were self-evident. Mill tried to "prove" that because we **desire** happiness, Utilitarianism is therefore "**desirable**" as a moral philosophy. But "happiness" is not inevitably the same as "goodness" and Mill never really explains why we are obliged to bring about the happiness of others.

Mill's Politics

Mill was a classical liberal. All individuals should be as free as possible from interference, especially from governments. Individuals' lives are only worth living when they are allowed to express their individual potential. No one has the right to interfere with an individual's freedom, unless their own life or freedom is threatened.

AT FIRST, I WAS CONVINCED THAT *LAISSEZ-FAIRE* CAPITALIST ECONOMICS WOULD PRODUCE "THE GREATEST HAPPINESS OF THE GREATEST NUMBER", BUT IN LATER YEARS I WAS MORE SYMPATHETIC TO SOCIALIST IDEALS.

He was also an active campaigner for women's rights. He defended various minorities, often forced to conform by public prejudice.

Mill championed democracy and freedom of speech. Democracy encourages individuals to be mature independent citizens rather than obedient subjects. When many different opinions and ideas are expressed, those that are innovative, true and valuable will thrive.

Bertrand Russell

John Stuart Mill was Bertrand Russell's agnostic "godfather". **Bertrand Russell** (1872–1970) was born into an aristocratic family. His parents both died when he was very young and he was raised by his severe grandmother. He went to Trinity College, Cambridge and quickly proved himself to be a brilliant mathematician.

I BECAME CONVINCED THAT MATHEMATICS IS SOMEHOW REDUCIBLE TO LOGIC.

He spent many years trying to prove this was so, unsuccessfully. Russell was also politically active all his life. He was imprisoned for protesting about compulsory conscription during the First World War and campaigned against nuclear weapons in the 1950s and 60s. He is probably the last great philosopher to believe that epistemology and perception must be the central problems of philosophy.

Relative Perception

Russell accepted most of the doctrines of British Empiricism. He thought it was very possible that the consistencies of our sensory experiences are caused by physical objects. But these experiences are all we can ever correctly claim to know. Different people have different sensory experiences of the world, which suggests that all empirical knowledge is inescapably relative.

MY PERCEPTIONS OF A ROOM WILL DIFFER FROM YOURS, BECAUSE OF WHERE WE BOTH STAND, AND HOW THE ROOM IS LIT, AND SO ON.

Sense Data

What we experience are sensations or what Russell (after **G.E. Moore** (1873 –1958)) called "sense data" – all the colours, shapes, textures, smells and sounds of the room.

G.E. Moore

SO THERE IS NO "REAL" ROOM AND IT HAS NO "TRUE" COLOUR.

THEY ARE "DATA" BECAUSE THEY ARE TRULY INFORMATIVE, AND BECAUSE THEY ARE "GIVEN".

SENSE DATA ARE INVOLUNTARY PHENOMENA THAT ARE BEYOND OUR CONTROL.

And although it is impossible to say whether there are physical objects, like rooms, at least sense data themselves are indubitable.

Russell's Theory of Knowledge

According to Russell, we are directly "acquainted" only with sense data, not objects.

SO, ANY KNOWLEDGE WE HAVE OF "ROOMS", FOR EXAMPLE, IS FALLIBLE, BECAUSE PHYSICAL OBJECTS ARE ONLY "LOGICAL CONSTRUCTIONS" INFERRED FROM SENSE DATA.

SUCH DERIVATIVE KNOWLEDGE I CALL "KNOWLEDGE BY DESCRIPTION".

We also have "knowledge by acquaintance" of other internal mental phenomena, like memories, beliefs and doubts, and, rather oddly, general ideas like "whiteness", "brotherhood" and "difference". So all knowledge by description ultimately depends on knowledge by acquaintance.

Logical Atomism

Most empiricist philosophers have always had an analytical or "atomist" approach to knowledge. The way to examine human knowledge is to break it down into elemental components like "simple ideas" or "impressions" and then see how complex ideas and knowledge systems relate to these fundamental knowledge "particles". If you can do this, then you should have a better understanding of what you are talking about. Russell's "logical atomism" is a complex version of this formula and is a theory of knowledge and meaning.

Russell's atoms appear to be "logical" in the sense that complex facts can be constructed from them.

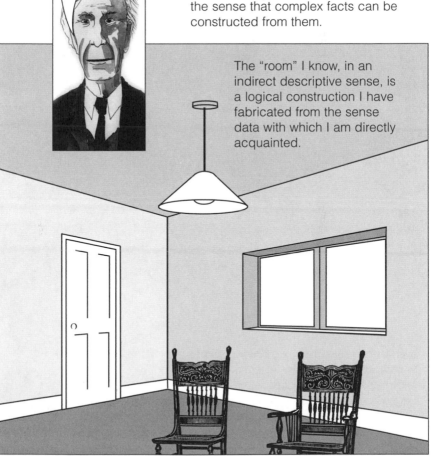

THE WORLD IS MADE UP OF "LOGICAL ATOMS" LIKE SENSE DATA, AS WELL AS PREDICATES, OR RELATIONS AND SO ON, AND THE FACTS COMPOSED OF THESE ATOMS.

The "room" I know, in an indirect descriptive sense, is a logical construction I have fabricated from the sense data with which I am directly acquainted.

Meaning and Atomic Facts

Sense data themselves are also puzzlingly both **objective** (because they are "given") and **subjective** (in the mind). Russell suggests that they are therefore neither, but rather "**neutral**" entities. "Atomic facts" about the world are also elementary and contain no logical connectives.

"THIS IS BLACK" STATES AN ATOMIC FACT ...

BUT "THIS IS BLACK OR GREY" DOESN'T.

ULTIMATELY, ALL LINGUISTIC MEANING IS DERIVED FROM THESE FUNDAMENTAL "ATOMS" AND "FACTS".

It's an extremely complex (and sometimes obscure) theory which was partly derived from the earlier work of his own student, **Ludwig Wittgenstein** (1889–1951), who was also trying to establish how it is that language has meaning. But, ultimately, Russell's complex empiricist theory of meaning remains unsatisfactory.

Mathematics and Logic

Not many philosophers now think that Russell's empiricist philosophy of meaning is very important. He will probably be best remembered for his earlier work *Principia Mathematica* (1910–13) undertaken with the philosopher **A.N. Whitehead** (1861–1947).

IT WAS A HUGE EXHAUSTING WORK THAT TOOK NINE YEARS TO COMPLETE ...

BUT OUR ATTEMPT TO PROVE THAT MATHEMATICS IS REDUCIBLE TO LOGIC WAS NOT SUCCESSFUL!

PRINCIPIA MATHEMATICA
TO *56

BY
ALFRED NORTH WHITEHEAD
AND
BERTRAND RUSSELL, F.R.S.

CAMBRIDGE
AT THE UNIVERSITY PRESS

In his efforts to achieve this, Russell made important contributions to the now diverse and complex subject of symbolic logic, mainly by showing how logic itself could be mathematized. His famous essay *On Denoting* (1905) led many modern philosophers to believe that philosophy has to be dedicated exclusively to "analytic activity", that is, deconstructing ordinary language in order to reveal its true "logical form". Perhaps this was Russell's chief legacy to modern 20th-century philosophy.

A.J. Ayer and the Vienna Circle

The last great British empiricist philosopher, so far, is **A.J. Ayer** (1910–89). His most famous work, *Language, Truth and Logic* (1936), appears "modern" because it focuses almost exclusively on language and meaning. Ayer travelled to Vienna in the early 1930s where he met with "The Vienna Circle".

WE WERE SCIENTISTS RATHER THAN PHILOSOPHERS.

WE THOUGHT THAT KNOWLEDGE COULD COME ONLY FROM SYSTEMATIC AND SCIENTIFIC INVESTIGATIONS OF THE WORLD.

THIS WAS AN EXTRAORDINARY GROUP OF OPTIMISTIC RADICALS KNOWN AS "LOGICAL POSITIVISTS".

Ayer returned to England, clutching various radical manifestos, convinced that Logical Positivism was a radical restatement of traditional British Empiricism.

Rudolf Carnap
(1891–1970)

Otto Neurath
(1882–1945)

Moritz Schlick
(1882–1936)

IT WAS THE WORLD ITSELF WHICH MARKED OUT THE BOUNDARIES OF HUMAN KNOWLEDGE.

Meaning and Logical Positivism

The Logical Positivists insisted that there could be no such thing as "philosophical knowledge". Modern philosophy could only ever be a useful "second-order" discipline which employed symbolic logic to analyse concepts, sort out linguistic confusions and "dissolve" all the pseudo-problems of traditional philosophy. One Logical Positivist slogan was "The meaning of a proposition is its method of verification". This means that all propositions have to explain how their content can be made testable, in practice or theory.

"THERE IS A DEPOSIT OF IRON ORE 500 FEET BELOW WHERE I AM SITTING" IS THEORETICALLY TESTABLE AND MAKES SENSE.

BUT "GOD CREATED THE WORLD" IS NOT AND IS THEREFORE NONSENSE.

The young Ayer was radical, optimistic and confident. He was convinced that "The Verification Principle" showed how most theology, metaphysics and ethics was deceptive nonsense, masquerading as sense.

Language Bewitchment

Empiricist philosophers have always been suspicious about the ability of language to mislead and betray. Bacon, Hobbes, Locke, Berkeley and Hume all agreed that language can persuade philosophers to believe in non-existent entities like "substance". The verification principle now revealed all talk about such things to be nonsense.

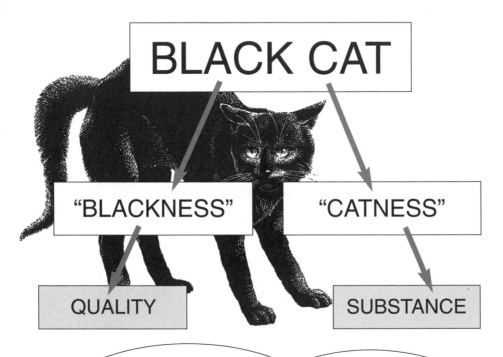

BLACK CAT

"BLACKNESS"

"CATNESS"

QUALITY

SUBSTANCE

THE INFAMOUS PROBLEM OF "SUBSTANCE" ARISES BECAUSE OF THE ASSUMPTION THAT THE STRUCTURE OF ORDINARY LANGUAGE MIRRORS HOW THE WORLD IS CONSTRUCTED.

JUST BECAUSE EVERYDAY LANGUAGE CONSISTS OF ADJECTIVES AND NOUNS, IT DOESN'T FOLLOW THAT THE WORLD CONSISTS OF CORRESPONDING QUALITIES AND SUBSTANCES.

Language "bewitchment" creates all sorts of complex philosophical "problems" which logical analysis reveals to be futile.

The Isness of Is

The verb "to be" in all its forms has always encouraged philosophers to think that certain entities have a kind of existence which they don't.

THE "IS" OF "THE UNICORN IS IN THE WOOD" MAKES NO EXISTENCE CLAIMS. IT MERELY JOINS TWO IDEAS TOGETHER.

"THE CAT IS A MAMMAL" REALLY MEANS SOMETHING LIKE "THE CLASS OF MAMMALS CONTAINS THE CLASS OF CATS", AND SO ON, IN STATEMENTS OF FACT.

Ayer's Phenomenalism

Ayer was another phenomenalist. He agreed with Mill and Russell that perception had to be analysed in terms of minds and sense data. The existence of physical objects is unprovable and their true nature unknowable. Phenomenalism doubts whether material objects exist independently of an observer or that they are necessarily the cause of our experiences.

So whenever we fall asleep, objects cease to exist as actual experiences and become merely possible ones.

It's a very odd set of beliefs which Ayer converted into a rather less alarming linguistic doctrine.

ALL *STATEMENTS* ABOUT PHYSICAL OBJECTS SHOULD BE TRANSLATED INTO "LOGICALLY EQUIVALENT" STATEMENTS ABOUT SENSE DATA, BOTH ACTUAL AND POSSIBLE.

But Ayer soon recognized that any "sense data language" would be impossibly prolix, and would inevitably smuggle in "physical object language" whenever it referred to "grass-like" data or the existence of potential observers.

The A Priori Tautologies

The a priori or deductive propositions of logic and mathematics have always worried empiricist philosophers because they seem to be mysteriously "self confirming". They aren't made true by any kind of observation or verification and appear to be a kind of "free lunch". Mill insisted they didn't exist. But most empiricists grudgingly accept them by demystifying their importance. Ayer thought that the propositions of mathematics had "meaning", but that mathematical truths themselves were just empty "tautologies".

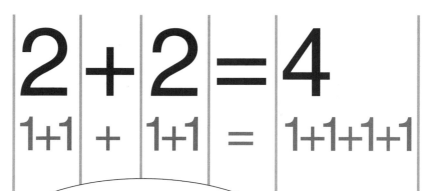

$$2+2=4$$
$$1+1 + 1+1 = 1+1+1+1$$

MATHEMATICS IS "ANALYTIC". 2+2=4 TELLS YOU NOTHING FRESH ABOUT THE WORLD, OR ABOUT ANYTHING OTHER THAN ITSELF.

IT IS JUST A CONVENIENT WAY OF TELLING YOU THAT 1+1+1 = 1+1+1.

Logic, similarly, is an empty verbal phenomenon. The obvious truth of "All bachelors are unmarried" depends on our understanding of the meaning and function of the words "bachelor" and "unmarried" and that is all. We know that whatever has shape has size, because of our understanding of the meanings and implications of terms like "shape" and "size".

Is This Correct?

"Everything that is red is coloured" is true only because of the meaning of words like "everything", "red" and "coloured". But is this correct? Some philosophers say that human language must have evolved to reflect a reality that lies behind it. The elementary "laws" of logic must reflect the fundamental nature of reality itself, or the limits of human understanding, or both.

The truth of these laws of logic predates language altogether.

The American pragmatist philosopher **W.V. Quine** (1908–2000) maintained that the Humean habit of dividing propositions into two kinds ("testable" ones and "self-confirming" ones) is itself an empiricist "dogma" that needs to be challenged. They are different in degree but not kind.

ALL OTHER KNOWLEDGE

EMBEDDED RULES AND LAWS

> PERHAPS SOME LAWS, RULES AND PROPOSITIONS ARE DEEPLY "EMBEDDED" IN OUR KNOWLEDGE SYSTEMS AND MAKE ALL OUR OTHER KNOWLEDGE POSSIBLE. THAT'S WHY WE TEND TO THINK OF THEM AS "SELF-CONFIRMING".

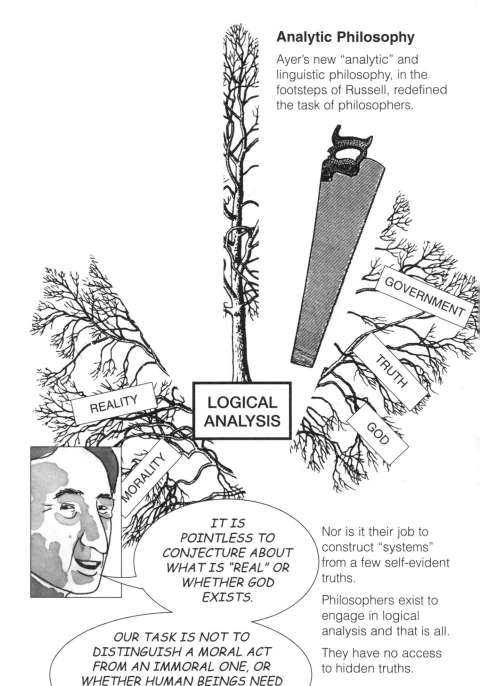

Analytic Philosophy

Ayer's new "analytic" and linguistic philosophy, in the footsteps of Russell, redefined the task of philosophers.

GOVERNMENT

TRUTH

GOD

REALITY

LOGICAL ANALYSIS

MORALITY

IT IS POINTLESS TO CONJECTURE ABOUT WHAT IS "REAL" OR WHETHER GOD EXISTS.

OUR TASK IS NOT TO DISTINGUISH A MORAL ACT FROM AN IMMORAL ONE, OR WHETHER HUMAN BEINGS NEED DEMOCRATIC GOVERNMENTS OR NOT.

Nor is it their job to construct "systems" from a few self-evident truths.

Philosophers exist to engage in logical analysis and that is all.

They have no access to hidden truths.

135

What of Religion?

The Logical Positivists were mostly hostile to organized religion which they associated with superstition, intolerance and war. The analysis of theological and religious language reveals it to be "nonsense".
"A benevolent God will save our souls" is impossible to verify or test. So Ayer agreed with Hume.

THEOLOGY IS NEARLY ALL SOPHISTRY AND ILLUSION AND SHOULD BE COMMITTED TO THE FLAMES.

BUT THEOLOGIANS ARGUE THAT RELIGIOUS LANGUAGE IS UNLIKE THE LANGUAGE OF SCIENCE. ITS FUNCTION IS NOT TO STATE EMPIRICAL FACTS.

Other philosophers criticize the Verificationist theory of meaning for being too restrictive and stipulative. People use language in all sorts of different ways, for all sorts of purposes and reasons, and not many of them would agree that what they say is "mostly nonsense".

And Ethics?

Similarly, ethical language cannot be factual, so it cannot be verified. That seems to make it a special kind of nonsense. Hume had claimed that a statement like "War is wrong" is really the statement of a report on individual feelings ("I dislike war"). Ayer famously insisted, in his Emotivist Theory, that ethical propositions were even more primitive – irrational outpourings of emotion.

> SAYING "WAR IS WRONG" IS MERELY THE EXPRESSION OF FEELINGS ...

> "WAR – BOO!"

But declaring your passions is surely not the only function of moral language.

Emotivism seems to rule out any calm or exploratory discussions about moral issues, and doesn't explain why there is so much agreement about many of them.

The philosopher **R.M. Hare** (1919–2002) thought that moral statements seem to function more like universal orders. The statement "WAR IS WRONG" should be reconstructed as ...

DON'T GO TO WAR, AND THIS MEANS YOU!

Problems with Verificationism

Ayer's verificationist account of meaning soon came under attack.

IN 1979, I CONFESSED THAT NEARLY ALL OF IT WAS FALSE.

THE VERIFICATION PRINCIPLE COULD NOT ITSELF BE VERIFIED OR MADE TESTABLE ...

SO IT TOO WAS NONSENSE.

Ayer found it impossible to formulate the Principle so that statements about *unverifiable* neutrons, quarks, scientific "models" and inductive generalizations could have meaning, whereas statements about ghosts, souls and God could not. Modern science is frequently abstract, complex, hypothetical and holistic, and does not always provide isolated factual assertions that can be verified by observation. Meaning also seems to be prior to verification. How can you verify statements which you know to be nonsensical – until they are verified?

Ayer's Theory of Meaning

Empiricist philosophers, including Ayer, have always been attracted to "referential" theories of meaning. Words have meaning because they somehow "point" to objects in the world or ideas in the mind. Both Russell and Ayer were persuaded (partly by the early work of Wittgenstein) that once language and reality were "atomized" (broken down to their most basic components in the form of elementary logical propositions and correlating "sense data"), then the problem of meaning would be explained and solved.

BUT TO "REDUCE" EVERYTHING TO ITS MOST PRIMITIVE CONSTITUENTS DOESN'T ALWAYS EXPLAIN MUCH.

THE BEST WAY TO UNDERSTAND A WATCH IS TO SEE IT WORKING AND TO OBSERVE HOW PEOPLE USE IT, NOT TO BREAK IT UP INTO PIECES.

Human beings convey meaning in many different ways. Not all of their communications can be "broken down" logically. So verification may be a sensible scientific procedure, useful for determining what is testable, but of little use as a general theory of meaning.

Meaning as Use

Wittgenstein concluded that it was absurd to look for any "one big thing" that gives language its meaning.

Language can also mislead philosophers into hopeless quests for entities that do not exist. Just because there are useful words like "art", "goodness" and "meaning" does not mean that they need a one-to-one relationship with some entity to generate meaning. Unlike truth, meaning seems to have little to do with what words or sentences refer to and what is observable or not.

The Doctrine Examined

This book began by explaining how philosophers have always given the word "know" a rather special and unusual meaning.

WE CAN ONLY EVER TRULY "KNOW" THOSE THINGS THAT ARE ABSOLUTELY CERTAIN, BEYOND ALL POSSIBLE DOUBT.

FOR PLATO THIS ABSOLUTE CERTAINTY COULD ONLY BE FOUND IN MATHEMATICS AND HIS MYSTERIOUS ARCHETYPAL "FORMS".

DESCARTES AND HUME CLAIMED DIFFERENTLY ...

ALL WE CAN REALLY KNOW IS THAT WE ARE THINKING.

MOST OF OUR FIRMLY HELD BELIEFS ARE BASED ON CUSTOM AND HABIT.

Many 20th-century philosophers now question this endless, and perhaps doomed, philosophical quest for absolute certainty. (Much depends on how you define words like "know", "doubt" and "certain".)

Knowledge Claims

Empiricist philosophy is primarily epistemological – concerned with the problem of knowledge. It declares that the most obvious and important source of knowledge is perception. This is why it remains mostly hostile to those claims made for other sources of knowledge like "reason" or "intuition".

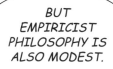

> BUT EMPIRICIST PHILOSOPHY IS ALSO MODEST.

> IT RARELY MAKES CLAIMS TO A KNOWLEDGE OF HIDDEN REALITIES OR PROFOUND METAPHYSICAL TRUTHS.

> WE CANNOT EVEN PROVE THAT PHYSICAL OBJECTS EXIST.

So it is necessarily unambitious. It recognizes that we have either a very limited or no contact with the "external" world. This restraint is also an attempt to make its foundations immune from sceptical doubt.

The Foundations of Empiricism

So what are the foundational certainties of empiricism? Our senses deceive us.

I THOUGHT THAT THE GREY VERTICAL SHAPE I SAW BEFORE ME, IN THE MIST, WAS A MAN, BUT IT WAS A STONE PILLAR.

BUT WHAT I CANNOT DOUBT IS THAT I HAD THE CONSCIOUS EXPERIENCE OF A GREY VERTICAL SHAPE, EVEN IF I WAS WHOLLY WRONG ABOUT WHAT CAUSED IT.

WE CANNOT BE MISTAKEN ABOUT WHAT WE *SEEM* TO SEE.

Empiricists drastically reduce their knowledge claims by settling for a knowledge of **appearances**.

There is a red, round shape in my consciousness, but I refuse to infer from that information that there is a cricket ball in my immediate field of vision. But at least I can be totally certain about this primitive red and round sense data. And my belief in the veracity of this sense data does not depend on any of my other beliefs, and so it is somehow "basic".

Images as Sense Knowledge

The doctrine of sense data is crucially important to all varieties of empiricism, representational, idealist or phenomenalist. Empiricists argue that "impressions" or sense data are "foundational" because they are exactly as they appear, with no hidden depths, which makes our knowledge of them incorrigible. We can never be wrong about sense data, or make mistakes about them.

THIS MAKES THEM A VERY ODD KIND OF "KNOWLEDGE", RATHER LIKE IMAGES ON A PHOTOGRAPHIC PLATE WHICH ARE ALSO ALWAYS "CORRECT".

A fact which has led some philosophers to say that to talk about "knowing" private experiences like these is misconceived. If sense data can never be questioned or doubted then they can't really be thought of as "knowledge" at all.

The Knowledge Building

But are sense data as reliable as Empiricists believe them to be? Do sense data have the sort of existence that is claimed for them? Does knowledge actually need some utterly infallible base on which to build?

145

What Does Science Tell Us?

The most convincing argument for the existence of sense data still relies on what science tells us about the physiological processes of perception. Light passes through the lens of the eye and gets focussed on the retina, electrical signals pass down along nerve fibres to those areas of the brain that specialize in sight, and then, somehow, we get a picture of the outside world in our minds.

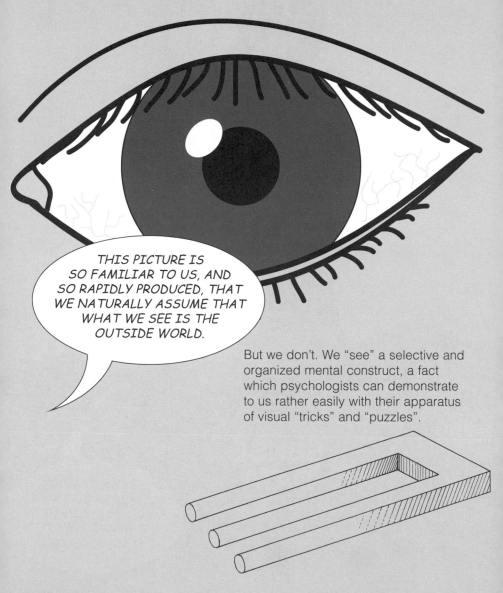

THIS PICTURE IS SO FAMILIAR TO US, AND SO RAPIDLY PRODUCED, THAT WE NATURALLY ASSUME THAT WHAT WE SEE IS THE OUTSIDE WORLD.

But we don't. We "see" a selective and organized mental construct, a fact which psychologists can demonstrate to us rather easily with their apparatus of visual "tricks" and "puzzles".

The Person Inside the Head

We see with "our minds", although it rarely seems like that. Exactly how we do it remains extremely mysterious, but our experiences of the external world are undoubtedly indirect. Perhaps because the end processes of perception remain so mysterious, empiricist philosophers are fond of talking about perception in terms of internal cinema screens or televisions.

AS IF THINKING AND EXPERIENCING WERE DONE BY A SMALL INDIVIDUAL "ME" VIEWING AN INTERNAL SCREEN.

But that only removes the mystery of perception to yet one more superfluous level and actually explains very little.

147

The Argument from Observer Relativity

The rather less impressive philosophical arguments for the existence of sense data depend mostly on the existence of illusions and hallucinations and the fact of observer relativity. Many people have had sensory experiences which are wrong, or for which there is no relevant physical object present. I see mirages in the desert.

Some see it as a brown rectangle, others as a black parallelogram, and so on. There is no way of knowing which (if any) of these experiences is the "real" colour or "real" shape of the table. People see images that are false, non-existent, or one out of many. The conclusion philosophers then draw is that all our experiences are internal mental phenomena.

Questions of Reliability

Such philosophical arguments for the existence of ideas or sense data usually rely on exaggerating the unreliability of a few sensory experiences and inferring from these that all our experiences are indirect and equally illusory.

BUT WE RARELY CONFUSE HALLUCINATIONS OR DREAMS ...

...WITH WAKING EXPERIENCES.

JUST BECAUSE WE OCCASIONALLY "MISPERCEIVE" DOES NOT AUTOMATICALLY IMPLY THAT ADDITIONAL MENTAL PHENOMENA ARE ALWAYS INVOLVED IN OUR PERCEPTIONS.

Illusions and hallucinations may consist of untrustworthy mental images, but that doesn't prove that the majority of our experiences are similarly "internal". After all, we only know that certain experiences were unreliable from the evidence of later more "reliable" observations. Nevertheless, we have no guarantee that one of these observations is true, beyond all possible doubt.

A Private World of Representations

The world may not be much like our perceptions of it. We are trapped in a private world of representations, or worse, a private world which tells us absolutely nothing about our immediate surroundings. Our sensory experiences may be caused by physical objects, or they may exist independent of any external stimuli. We can, if we want, infer from them to a world of physical objects.

But the more we examine the processes of perception, the more uncertainty there is about what exactly it is that we are perceiving. This uncertainty helps to explain why empiricist philosophers rather desperately cling to the supposed indubitability of internal ideas, impressions and sense data.

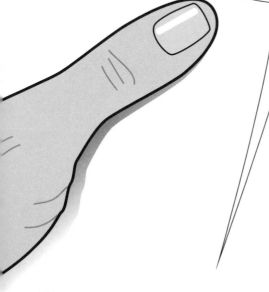

I MAY NOT BE ABLE TO PROVE THAT THIS BOOK EXISTS, BUT I CAN AT LEAST BE CERTAIN OF THE BOOK-LIKE SENSE DATA IN MY MIND.

By claiming to know so very little, empiricists feel that they are on safe ground.

How Real Are Sense Data?

But the ontological (reality) status of sense data remains very puzzling. Are sense data mental or physical phenomena, or somehow both or neither? Are they states of mind or objects in their own right? If they are objects, how temporary or permanent are they? Are they private or public? If they are private, then presumably there are as many sense data as there are observers.

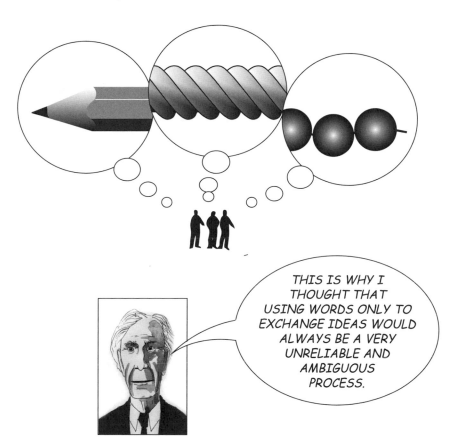

THIS IS WHY I THOUGHT THAT USING WORDS ONLY TO EXCHANGE IDEAS WOULD ALWAYS BE A VERY UNRELIABLE AND AMBIGUOUS PROCESS.

Are phenomenalists right to say that ideas exist when unperceived? If they exist as "possible experiences", how do they? (Most phenomenalists give up on this one, and claim that the odd half-life of unperceived sense data is just a fundamental fact about how things are.) And if all we ever experience is sense data, then the existence of other people with minds is also open to doubt.

The Adverbial Solution

One attempt to eliminate these problems about sense data is to suggest that we should think of perception as "adverbial".

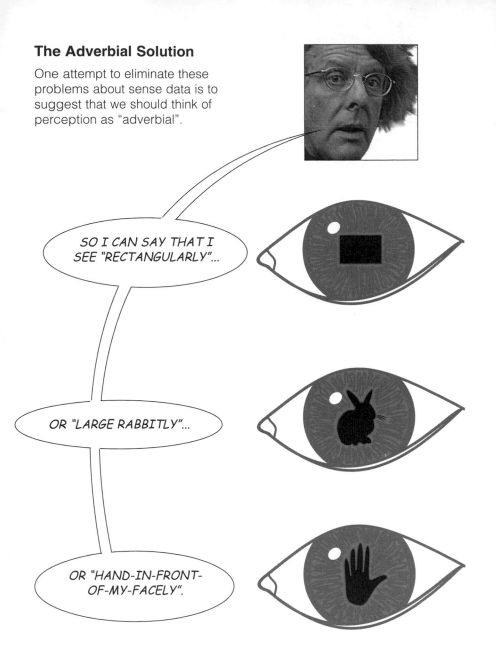

SO I CAN SAY THAT I SEE "RECTANGULARLY"...

OR "LARGE RABBITLY"...

OR "HAND-IN-FRONT-OF-MY-FACELY".

This avoids all references to mysterious sense data. But it doesn't really explain much about the nature of perception itself. Or how certain we can be about our experiences.

Perceptions as Beliefs

Or perhaps we should think of perception as being more like beliefs and judgements that sometimes go wrong.

BUT PERCEPTION AND BELIEF ARE HARDLY THE SAME THING.

WE ACQUIRE BELIEFS BECAUSE OF OUR EXPERIENCES.

Beliefs are much more complex than perception and can be expressed linguistically.

So we may be stuck with sense data as the best explanation after all.

153

Immediacy

We've also seen how virtually all empiricist philosophy, from Locke onwards, depends on the primacy of these ideas, impressions or sense data. They are the unshakeable truth on which empiricist philosophy is based.

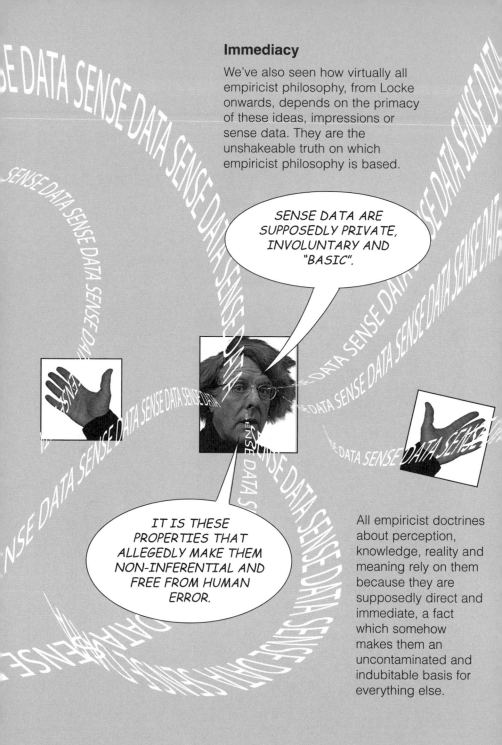

> SENSE DATA ARE SUPPOSEDLY PRIVATE, INVOLUNTARY AND "BASIC".

> IT IS THESE PROPERTIES THAT ALLEGEDLY MAKE THEM NON-INFERENTIAL AND FREE FROM HUMAN ERROR.

All empiricist doctrines about perception, knowledge, reality and meaning rely on them because they are supposedly direct and immediate, a fact which somehow makes them an uncontaminated and indubitable basis for everything else.

Looking and Seeing

But, on the surface, our experience of the physical world doesn't seem to be at all inferential or "indirect". Our perception of physical objects seems immediate – as if through a pane of glass.

Whatever the inferential process consists of, it is rapid and usually unconscious. So how exactly sense data actually are more "direct" or "immediate" remains unclear.

Logical and Psychological Processes

Empiricist philosophers would say that even though we are utterly unaware of the mental processes involved, this does not mean they do not occur. It is important that we do not confuse our lack of psychological awareness with the logical truth that all perception remains mediated and inferential.

It seems as if it is the existence of sense data themselves that has to be inferred. We must assume that they exist, if the scientific accounts of perception are correct, even though we seem to have no conscious experience of them (except for a few infrequent illusions and hallucinations, perhaps).

What Do We See?

This may mean that the philosophical importance and ontological status of sense data are not very great, and their certainty questionable.

If our hypothetical experiences of sense data are not qualitatively different from our more conscious direct experience of physical objects, do we need them at all?

The Private Language Argument

Descartes and most British Empiricist philosophers assumed, without question, that the only way to construct a system of knowledge is to begin with a few private thoughts or experiences about which they could be wholly certain. (Like "I am thinking" or "I am experiencing a red sensation".) The private is supposedly better known than the public.

I CAN DESCRIBE AND EXPRESS MY PRIVATE IDEAS AND EXPERIENCES TO MYSELF, WITHOUT PRESUPPOSING THE EXISTENCE OF ANY EXTERNAL WORLD OR OTHER MINDS.

ONCE THESE PRIVATE BUT CERTAIN FOUNDATIONS HAVE BEEN ESTABLISHED, THEN I CAN BUILD FROM THE INSIDE OUT ...

I can rely on inferences to make less certain conclusions about everything else. So philosophical knowledge begins with inner private sensations and constructs a more public knowledge from that platform.

Public Language

But our thoughts and experiences can only ever be conceptualized or described in a language that is social and public. As soon as we think, we are doing so in a *shared* language, derived from a specific culture with a particular history. It seems very unlikely that we construct some peculiarly "private" language that names our private ideas.

Wittgenstein's Criticism

Wittgenstein's "private language argument" is itself complex and not always clear, and its implications endlessly debated. It is primarily an attack on Russell's general theory of language which suggested that language gets its meaning from a direct "acquaintance" with sense data. Wittgenstein's argument goes something like this …

RULES ARE MEANINGLESS UNLESS THERE IS SOME WAY OF CHECKING TO SEE IF A RULE HAS BEEN APPLIED CORRECTLY.

THIS CHECK MUST BE A PUBLIC CHECK.

IF WE WERE TO GIVE A TERM MEANING BY POINTING TO AN INNER PRIVATE EXPERIENCE AND THEN USED THE SAME TERM LATER ON, WE COULD NEVER KNOW IF WE WERE USING THAT TERM CORRECTLY.

Language always serves a *function*. We have to learn the words for tastes, colours, smells and dreams, however private the sensations they describe. The notion of a "private language" unique to one individual makes no sense. It is impossible therefore to name private sensations in the way that empiricists claim, and the project for some sort of pure non-inferential sense data "language" is wholly misconceived.

Several other criticisms also seem to flow from Wittgenstein's conclusions about language, ideas and knowledge. The "private room" model of the mind that empiricists mostly leave unexamined is open to serious doubt. Communication between individuals does not seem to involve the transference of imagery from one mind into another.

Thinking is not about "looking inside" our minds. We do not "see" our thoughts and then express them verbally.

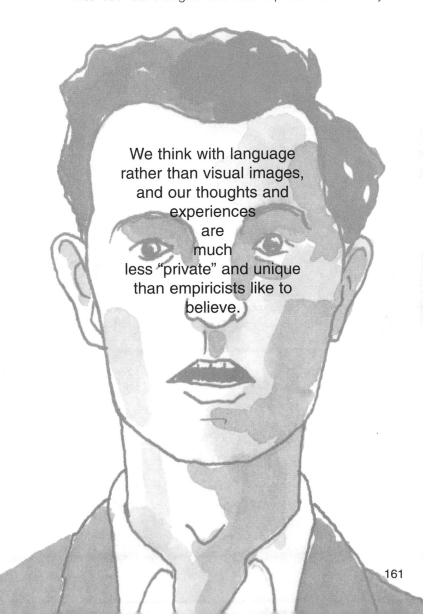

We think with language rather than visual images, and our thoughts and experiences are much less "private" and unique than empiricists like to believe.

The Outside Within Experience

Wittgenstein thought that "sense data" might well exist, but not in the forms imagined by empiricist philosophers. He also suggested they were, anyway, of little philosophical importance. It is our conceptual structures which largely determine how we see the world and these are primarily linguistic.

THERE IS NO WORLD OF PRIVATE EXPERIENCES FROM WHICH WE CAN "BUILD OUTWARDS".

EMPIRICIST PHILOSOPHY CLAIMS THAT WE LEARN EVERYTHING FROM EXPERIENCE ...

LANGUAGE CULTURE

... DETACHED FROM THE VERY LANGUAGE AND CULTURE THAT MAKE US HUMAN.

... AND YET WANTS TO BEGIN FROM A POSITION OF TOTAL ISOLATION ...

If all we ever had was access to a series of disconnected, unconceptualized private experiences, then we could never acquire knowledge at all. We can only have experiences after we are socialized beings. Empiricist philosophy now seems much odder and more incoherent than it did at first.

Knowledge in the World

Another great 20th-century philosopher, **Karl Popper** (1902–94), also attacked the "first person" doctrines of empiricist epistemology which claim that knowledge must begin with subjective experiences. Knowledge, says Popper, is best envisaged as an evolutionary process that advances through problem solving. The objective world of material things exists, as well as subjective minds.

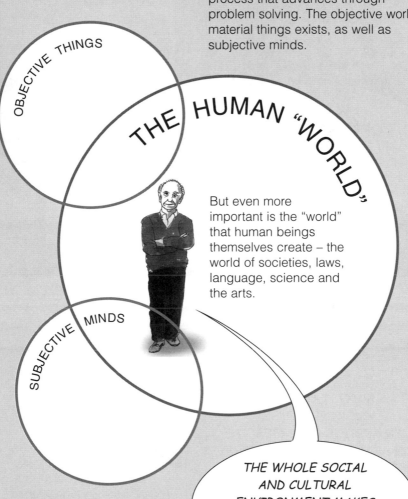

OBJECTIVE THINGS

THE HUMAN "WORLD"

SUBJECTIVE MINDS

But even more important is the "world" that human beings themselves create – the world of societies, laws, language, science and the arts.

THE WHOLE SOCIAL AND CULTURAL ENVIRONMENT MAKES HUMANS INTO THE UNIQUE BEINGS THEY ARE.

The Power of Knowledge

Knowledge has to be a public and objective construct – found in libraries rather than individual minds, open to free debate and criticism, independent of any knowing subject.

KNOWLEDGE CANNOT MERELY BE SOMETHING BUILT UP FROM INTERNAL SENSORY EXPERIENCES.

Radical "postmodernist" philosophers like **Michel Foucault** (1926–84) further insist that knowledge is always a social and political construct.

WHAT COUNTS AS KNOWLEDGE, THE CATEGORIES IT CREATES, THE ACCESS IT PROVIDES OR DENIES, THE KIND OF SOCIAL AND POLITICAL REALITIES IT CREATES ARE ALL DETERMINED BY THE POWERFUL.

"KNOWLEDGE" IS USED TO EXCLUDE AND CONTROL THOSE WHO ARE DENIED ACCESS TO ITS MEANS OF PRODUCTION.

TIME

Kant on Perception

Nevertheless, empiricist philosophers are probably right to insist that our experiences are always "mediated". In other words, an internal "model" of the world is what we experience and we have no way of knowing how closely that model approximates to "the world itself". Immanuel Kant felt forced, by the philosophical scepticism of Hume, to re-examine the whole problem of perception and experience.

THE HUMAN MIND MUST CONTAIN INNATE CAPACITIES OF A VERY SPECIFIC KIND ...

WE MUST THINK "CAUSALLY" ABOUT OBJECTS WITHIN A FRAMEWORK OF "TIME AND SPACE" – AND THESE ARE THE PRE-GIVEN CATEGORIES OF THE MIND.

The Kantian Categories

The mind applies concepts or "categories" to all our experiences in order for us to understand them and give them meaning. So causation, substance, space and time are not features that we read off from our experience of the world, but *preconditions for anything* to be an experience for us in the first place.

WHAT OUR MINDS CANNOT MEDIATE IN THIS WAY, CANNOT BE AN EXPERIENCE FOR US. IT CANNOT BE KNOWLEDGE.

SUBSTANCE

CAUSATION

TIME

SPACE

This means that any knowledge we have of the external world is even more irretrievably human.

Conceptual Frameworks

Most modern psychologists agree with Kant, although they use words like "frames of reference" and "perceptual sets" to describe what is going on. Our "visual fields" are never experienced directly, but are always instantly "conceptualized". (New-born babies and a few Impressionist artists may be the only people to ever see something like an unconceptualized world of raw sense data.) The rest of us apply concepts to our experiences instantly, so that they have meaning for us.

This suggests that empiricist models of perceptual processes are incorrect. There are no "first impressions" or "raw data". We do not "receive" information passively, but actively "create" our experiences. We do not draw inferences from sensory information, but impose meanings upon it.

I see a red ball.

PERCEPTION MAY BE MORE LIKE WRITING A NOVEL THAN WATCHING A CINEMA SCREEN.

Language reinforces this process, so that even our elementary experience of red colours may be "tainted" and narrowed because of our application of the word "red" itself.

167

Language and Experience

Language is what we think with and partly determines what we experience. Language is seriously corrupted with all kinds of presuppositions, ideologies, social constructs, beliefs and prejudices. So human perception must itself be irrepressibly contaminated. We select and create what we see according to our past experiences, motivation, education, culture, class, gender and subjection to various ideologies. When we see the "duck-rabbit", we do not experience it as raw data from which we draw inferences, but instantly see it as either a duck or a rabbit.

WE IMPOSE CONCEPTS OF "DUCK" OR "RABBIT" ONTO WHAT IS THERE, BUT SEEM UNABLE TO IMPOSE BOTH SIMULTANEOUSLY.

This doesn't mean that sense data do not exist, but it does imply that uncontaminated raw data in any form is rarely experienced directly or consciously.

Making Our World

We make the world, and the world makes us, in all sorts of interactive and reciprocal causal processes. It seems impossible for us to ever have any direct contact with the physical world. We see it in pictures which are monitored and controlled by fundamental categories and cultural frameworks. We are many times removed from the "raw data".

ALL OUR KNOWLEDGE ABOUT OUR SURROUNDINGS IS UTTERLY HUMAN AND FALLIBLE ...

... EVEN THOUGH, IN ITS PUBLIC FORMS, IT HAS HELPED US TO SURVIVE.

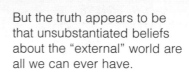

But the truth appears to be that unsubstantiated beliefs about the "external" world are all we can ever have.

Empiricism Denied

"She asked him what his father's books were about. 'Subject and object and the nature of reality,' Andrew had said. And when she said, Heavens, she had no notion of what that meant. 'Think of a kitchen table then,' he told her, 'when you're not there.'"

(*To the Lighthouse*, **Virginia Woolf** (1882–1941))

Nowadays there are few philosophers worrying away at the traditional problems of Empiricist philosophy, like the ontological status of unperceived furniture. Most of them would probably agree with Virginia Woolf's character, Lily Briscoe, that much British Empiricism is odd, narrow in its concerns and often rather pointless.

EMPIRICISM'S FUNDAMENTAL DOCTRINES MADE IT PECULIARLY UNSUITABLE AS A METHOD FOR INVESTIGATING LANGUAGE AND MEANING.

ITS LONG HELD ADMIRATION FOR "OBJECTIVE" SCIENTIFIC METHODS AND PROCEDURES NOW SEEMS NAIVE.

British and European Philosophy

Many of the key empiricist philosophers themselves are now mostly better known for other reasons. Locke is famous as one of the founders of political liberalism. Hume as a conceptual analyst and sceptic. Mill as a moral and political philosopher. Russell as a logician and political rebel. Empiricist philosophers are, sometimes unfairly, often accused of ignoring social, economic, political and cultural realities.

COMPLEX ARGUMENTS ABOUT "REAL" AND "APPARENT TABLES" NOW SEEM TRIVIAL COMPARED WITH THE RATHER MORE AMBITIOUS SUBJECT MATTERS PURSUED BY EUROPEAN PHILOSOPHERS ...

Immanuel Kant
(1724–1804)

G.W.F. Hegel
(1770–1831)

Friedrich Nietzsche
(1844–1900)

Karl Marx
(1818–83)

Martin Heidegger
(1889–1976)

Even Russell and Ayer seemed unable to escape from the entrenched doctrines of traditional empiricist dogma. It took "outsiders" like Wittgenstein and Popper to see what was wrong, to propose better ways of thinking about language, and to suggest other more important things to think about. But that's another story.

The Unknowable Mind

Wittgenstein teased out many of the absurdities that seem to be inevitable if we think of the mind as being like some kind of private room. Minds are necessarily more public, primarily because they think with a collective language. Nevertheless, materialist philosophers of mind are still puzzled and irritated by the fact that human minds and their experiences persist in remaining private and largely unknowable.

HUMAN EXPERIENCE STILL REMAINS INACCESSIBLE TO SCIENTIFIC INVESTIGATION.

CONSCIOUSNESS STILL RETAINS ITS ESSENTIALLY PRIVATE CHARACTER.

No matter how much we know about wave-lengths of light and human sensory perception, science seems unable to describe or explain the total uniqueness of our perceptual experiences or "qualia".

A Future for Empiricism?

Recent philosophers like **Richard Rorty** (b. 1931) may be right to argue that the inescapable autonomy of language means that it can never be anything like a "mirror" of reality and that meaning cannot possibly be derived from the world. Nevertheless, when the postmodernist sociologist **Jean Baudrillard** (b. 1929) claims that modern wars are media events, and so "do not happen", the desire to verify the meaning of his remarks against concrete experience becomes rather tempting.

> MEANING AND TRUTH MAY BE OUT THERE AFTER ALL, NOT FOREVER TRAPPED IN LANGUAGE AND IDEOLOGY.

> BUT I INSIST THAT MODERN PHILOSOPHY MUST LIMIT ITS AMBITIONS. IT CAN NEVER BE ANYTHING MORE THAN A SPECIAL KIND OF "CONVERSATION".

Rorty's claim agrees with British Empiricism which has always been a moderate enterprise of limited aspirations, suspicious of great philosophical systems or "grand narratives", and pessimistic about the extent of human knowledge.

No one has ever been harmed by it. So perhaps it may have a kind of limited future after all.

Further Reading

Below are listed most of the philosophical works referred to directly in this book. Empiricist philosophy is usually well written, which is why philosophy students are often introduced to the subject by studying its various forms. Reading Berkeley is always diverting, because even though you suspect he is talking something close to nonsense, his arguments are usually persuasive and very difficult to disprove. Hume's *Treatise* is more radical and immediate than his *Essay*. And Ayer's *Language, Truth and Logic*, although occasionally difficult, still reads like the work of a ruthless young rebel, determined to bring down all established beliefs and values.

Francis Bacon: the Major Works (Oxford World's Classics 2002)
Leviathan, Thomas Hobbes (Penguin Classics 1981)
The Elements of Law, Natural and Political, Thomas Hobbes (Oxford World's Classics 1999)
An Essay Concerning Human Understanding, John Locke (Oxford University Press Paperback 1979)
Two Treatises of Government, John Locke (Cambridge University Press 1960)
A New Theory of Vision and Other Writings, George Berkeley (Dent Everyman Paperback 1973)
The Principles of Human Knowledge and Three Dialogues, George Berkeley (Oxford World's Classics 1999)
A Treatise of Human Nature, David Hume (Oxford Philosophical Texts 2000)
An Enquiry Concerning Human Understanding and Concerning the Principles of Morals, David Hume (Oxford Philosophical Texts 1999)
Dialogues Concerning Natural Religion, David Hume (Oxford Paperback 1998)
Utilitarianism and Other Essays, Jeremy Bentham and John Stuart Mill (Penguin Classics 1987)
On Liberty and Other Essays, John Stuart Mill (Oxford World's Classics 1998)
The Subjection of Women, John Stuart Mill (Dover Paperback 1997)
The Problems of Philosophy, Bertrand Russell (Oxford University Press Paperback 2001)
Our Knowledge of the External World, Bertrand Russell (Routledge 1993)
Human Knowledge – its Scope and Limits, Bertrand Russell (Routledge 1992)
Language, Truth and Logic, A.J. Ayer (Pelican 1974)
The Foundations of Empirical Knowledge, A.J. Ayer (Macmillan 1940)
The Central Questions of Philosophy, A.J. Ayer (Pelican 1956)

Three books which provide a useful survey of Empiricist Philosophy are:

The British Empiricists, Stephen Priest (Penguin Books 1990)
The Empiricists, R.S. Woolhouse (Opus Books, Oxford University Press 1988)
Locke, Berkeley and Hume: Central Themes, Jonathan Bennett (Oxford University Press 1977)

Perception, Godfrey Vesey (Doubleday 1971) is a good introduction to the questions raised by the doctrine of "sense data".

The Past Masters Series of books

are always accessible. Others in this list sometimes are less so, although they are all illuminating.

Bacon, Anthony Quinton (Past Masters Series, Oxford University Press 1988)

Hobbes, R.S. Peters (Penguin 1956)

Perspectives on Thomas Hobbes, ed. G.A.J. Rogers and Alan Ryan (Oxford University Press 1988)

Locke, John Dunn (Past Masters Series, Oxford University Press 1984)

The Cambridge Companion to Locke, ed. Vere Chappell (Cambridge University Press 1994)

Locke, R.S. Woolhouse (Harvester Press 1983)

Problems from Locke, J.L. Mackie (Oxford University Press 1976)

Berkeley, J.O. Urmson (Past Masters Series, Oxford University Press 1982)

Berkeley, A.C. Grayling (Duckworth 1986)

Berkeley: The Philosophy of Immaterialism, I.C. Tipton (Methuen 1974)

Hume, A.J. Ayer (Past Masters Series, Oxford University Press 1980)

The Philosophy of David Hume, Norman Kemp Smith (London 1949)

The Cambridge Companion to Mill, ed. John Skorupski (Cambridge University Press 1998)

Bertrand Russell, John Watling (Oliver and Boyd 1970)

Ayer, John Foster (Routledge 1985)

Empiricist Philosophy has never really fully recovered from the attacks made upon it by these books, among others:

Sense and Sensibilia, J.L. Austin (Oxford University Press 1962)

From a Logical Point of View (Contains the essay 'Two Dogmas of Empiricism'), W.V.O. Quine (Harvard University Press 1961)

Philosophical Investigations, Ludwig Wittgenstein (Blackwell 1988)

Objective Knowledge: An Evolutionary Approach, Karl Popper (Oxford University Press Paperback 1972)

To the Lighthouse, Virginia Woolf (Penguin 1968) is not a critique of Empiricism as such, but does poke fun at the pretensions and foibles of philosophers and philosophy students.

Dave Robinson has taught Empiricist philosophy to his students for many years. Fortunately, only a few have ended up doubting the existence of physical objects. He has written several Icon books, including *Introducing Russell*.

The author is grateful for the support and advice of his stalwart editor, Richard Appignanesi, and the inventive and witty illustrations of Bill Mayblin. He also feels obliged to thank his partner, Judith, who provided him with a constant supply of tea, and recommended he read Virginia Woolf. His cat still exists as a set of possible sense experiences, in the room next door.

Bill Mayblin is the senior partner of Information Design Workshop, a London-based graphic design practice. He has illustrated several Icon books, including *Introducing Derrida*.

Index